PULL UP A CHAIR

Tiffani Thiessen

PULL UP A CHAIR

RECIPES FROM MY FAMILY TO YOURS

WITH RACHEL HOLTZMAN
PHOTOGRAPHY BY REBECCA SANABRIA

HOUGHTON MIFFLIN HARCOURT
Boston   New York

Copyright © 2018 by Tiffani
Thiessen Creative, Inc.

Photography © 2018 by
Rebecca Sanabria

For information about
permission to reproduce
selections from this book,
write to trade.permissions@
hmhco.com or to Permissions,
Houghton Mifflin Harcourt
Publishing Company, 3 Park
Avenue, 19th Floor, New York,
New York 10016.

hmhco.com

Library of Congress
Cataloging-in-Publication Data

Names: Thiessen, Tiffani, 1974–
author. | Holtzman, Rachel,
author.
Title: Pull up a chair : recipes
from my family to yours /
Tiffani Thiessen
with Rachel Holtzman.
Description: Boston : Houghton
Mifflin Harcourt, 2018. |
Includes index.
Identifiers: LCCN 2018001643
(print) | LCCN 2017059617
(ebook) | ISBN
9781328710390 (ebook) | ISBN
9781328710307 (paper over
board)
Subjects: LCSH: Cooking. |
LCGFT: Cookbooks.
Classification: LCC TX714
(print) | LCC TX714 .T4933 2018
(ebook) | DDC
641.5—dc23
LC record available at https://
lccn.loc.gov/2018001643

Cover and book design by
Shubhani Sarkar,
sarkardesignstudio.com

Printed in the United States

DOW 10 9 8 7 6 5 4 3 2
4500735911

To all the friends and family who make
my table my favorite place to be.

Holt, Harper, and Brady—
may your bellies always be full
and your hearts more so.

CONTENTS

INTRODUCTION

If your house is anything like mine, then you don't need me to tell you that we don't get together the way we used to. Meals—if you can call them that!—are eaten on the run; we text more than we talk; and connecting with our families for more than 10 minutes between school, work, appointments, lessons, housework, and homework is not always a reality. Sure, I might look all glammed up and pulled together on TV, but you better believe that there are days when putting on real pants is a major victory. Now that I have two kids of my own, I understand more than ever just how hard it is to get food on the table and to spend quality time together, not to mention with our loved ones and friends, too. Where did we all go?!

Growing up, my dad worked two jobs, and my mom was home with me and my two brothers, working her butt off raising us. We didn't have a lot of money, and we definitely didn't have a lot of time together, but we *always* had family dinner. I remember walking into the house after school, and it would smell like supper. I'd get a whiff of tomato sauce and think, *Dad's favorite!* Or smell beef stroganoff and think, *Ugh, no thanks.* (By the way, I've made it *so* much better with wild mushrooms, a splash of brandy, and creamy polenta . . . sorry, Mom.) But no matter what was on the table, it was an opportunity for us all to take a moment, feel seen and heard, and enjoy each other's company, even if just for a moment before we all scattered again.

I've tried to keep that come-together spirit alive in my own home. Okay, so maybe it's not *every* night—my husband has definitely been known to sneak my daughter out to McDonald's so I can have a few quiet moments with my toddler son (no judgment, please!)—and it's definitely not all perfectly pressed napkins and elaborate composed dishes every time I want to get people together. (Hello, DIY Pizza Party.) It's whatever we can make happen a few times a week so we can come back together again as a family, or with friends, neighbors, or whoever else happens to be in our house and with an appetite. *Pull up a chair*, we say.

It's the simplest sentiment, but it means so much. It's not just sitting down and eating; it's about reconnecting with the things that make us all so much *happier*. It's about laughter and joy and conversation. It's no coincidence that #PullUpAChair became the hashtag for my Cooking Channel show, *Dinner at Tiffani's*; and it seemed like a natural fit as the title for this book. After all, these two projects were born from the same idea: Offer delicious, relatable food that any home cook could make (there was no culinary school for this gal!), throw in some fun ideas for celebrations and gatherings, and serve up inspiration for getting the people you love around a table, whether it's over an unfussy weekday supper of Not-Your-Mama's Turkey Meat Loaf, a sunny-day picnic with Fried Chicken with Pickle & Potato Salad, or a lazy morning with Poached Egg Toasts with Kale. Oh yeah, and add a heaping side of silly—because no one should take food too seriously.

Sure, the guests on my show might be fancy-pants celebrities, but guess what? It doesn't get more real than people shoving delicious food in their faces. And I'm all about keeping things real. My love for cooking comes from the most honest, genuine place: watching my mom, aunt, and grandmother in the kitchen. Growing up, you could usually find me hanging out with them, helping make things like my mom's famous Cream Cheese Pie (the recipe for which this book would not be complete without). And ladies were the ones taking the lead on the grill during BBQ season. (I thought marrying a Texan would change that for me, but not so much!) These incredible women not only taught me how to put great flavors together, but also instilled in me how special it is to share a homemade meal, no matter how humble. I realized that

if I could bring people joy doing simple things like cooking up a Roasted Chicken Potpie, delivering a parcel of parchment-wrapped Sea Salt Chocolate Chip Cookies to a new neighbor, or hosting a Backyard Camp-Out—I could bring a little more of the good stuff into people's lives. And better yet, I could share what I learned with anyone else who wanted to do it too. *Pull Up a Chair* is all about the little touches that go such a long way, from getting a pot of Four-Bean Chili on the stove with a spread of (store-bought) toppings, to giving everyone a section of the newspaper at breakfast. (There's nothing like the cartoons or a crossword puzzle challenge to get your kids to sit at the table!) Or better yet, creating something handmade—a detail I always like to include—such as handwritten place cards or a hanging chalkboard with the meal's menu.

The best part? It doesn't take that much time—at least not with a little advanced planning. And have I mentioned that I'm a master planner? As a little girl, whenever my family was going on a trip, I would start packing and planning *weeks* in advance. What can I say? I was *that* kid. And since I started modeling and acting at eight years old, that planning and preparation came in handy. You had to know your lines, hit your marks, and make your flights. So I planned. I thrived on preparation and being ready. I realized that every little bit I could do ahead of time would allow me—and those around me—to better experience the process. The same goes for getting dinner on the table. Whether it's hosting a group of twenty for an elegant holiday feast or four for Tuesday-night dinner, the same rules apply: The more you can do ahead of time, the more you can enjoy yourself. And the more your guests can enjoy themselves too—there's no bigger party downer than a stressed-out host!

That's why, when it comes to cooking and hosting, I'm a huge fan of checklists, and I've included my go-to version for you to use too. Everything from groceries to prep to sending my husband out for the ice to getting the kids (and myself!) dressed to taking photographs of my gorgeous spread goes on the list. I've also included some of my favorite ideas for get-togethers, from a Mexi-Cali Fiesta to a classic Lobster Boil (or "Brady Boil," as I call it, since my husband is usually first in line to throw on a bib and hunker down). I'll help you think about things like décor and presentation, and recommend dishes from this book that come together to make the perfect menu. My hope is that it will make it as easy as possible for you to jump right into the party spirit—and see for yourself how a fun, special gathering is never further than a yummy spread (and maybe a cocktail) away.

Still not convinced you have enough time? Or that you'll enjoy cooking a homemade meal for your family? As I see it, it's all about making it a priority—even if it's just one night a week—and practicing. It's just like going to the gym; sometimes you don't want to go, but it's good for your body, your mind, and your soul. And the more you do it, the easier it gets. I promise I'll get you there! And while I'm at it, I'll give you my tips and tricks for the lazy gal's shortcuts, mixing homemade with store-bought, kid-friendly recipe tweaks, how to dress up a table (without driving yourself nuts), and no-sweat party ideas. You'll see that you don't need mad skills in the kitchen to make these recipes, enjoy doing it, and feel proud of getting people around your table.

So come on in, get comfortable, and, well, you know what to do. I'll save a seat for you.

xo *Tiffani*

RISE

AND

SHINE

was never much of a breakfast eater as a kid—my mom had to force me to sit down every morning and eat *something*, whether it was a bowl of cereal or a piece of fruit. As a teen, and even in my early twenties, I just never woke up feeling like I needed or wanted food. Well, that changed! Now it's one of my favorite meals of the day, namely because it's a time when I can get everyone around the table—for at least a few minutes—and know I'm sending them all off into the world with big, full bellies. It can be a total juggling act on some mornings, and sometimes it's not much more than eggs and toast (more later on why we're pretty much eating eggs every which way we can—hint: my husband has a chicken addiction), but

that moment when everyone has a plate of food in front of them feels like one where I can take a deep breath. There's nothing better than starting the day all together and nourishing our bodies for the busy time ahead.

Breakfast (and brunch) is also one of my favorite meals for entertaining. It's just begging for a seemingly endless spread heaped full of all kinds of dishes, both sweet and savory—especially great make-aheads like Scones (page 7) or Egg & Sausage Casserole (page 31)—plus fresh juices and fun morning-appropriate cocktails (hello, Bloody Caesar with Maple-Fennel Bacon, page 18). Other meals can be more intimate, but breakfast is for feeding a crowd of family or friends.

GREEN SMOOTHIES

There's no quicker way to get a lot of great vitamins into your body than with a fresh, homemade smoothie. By adding things like creamy, healthy fat–loaded avocado, nutrient-powerhouse spinach, and antioxidant-packed pineapple and mango, you have a meal—or snack—that's going to go the distance. It's the ultimate grab 'n' go. And if your kids are anything like mine and suspicious of all things green, I promise that after a sip, they'll never know they've been veg'd!

You can change up this recipe any way you like—swapping spinach for kale or pineapple and mango for berries. I call for frozen fruit here, but feel free to use fresh. You'll just want to add a few ice cubes to the mix.

Serves 4 to 6

1½ cups coconut water

1 cup packed fresh
spinach leaves

½ cup frozen diced pineapple

½ cup frozen diced mango

2 sprigs fresh mint leaves

¼ avocado, diced

Juice of 1 lime

In a blender, combine the coconut water, spinach, pineapple, mango, mint, avocado, and lime juice. Blend until smooth.

SCONES

Scones are one of my favorite things to make with my daughter, Harper. Baking in particular is great to do with kids—there are no sharp objects involved, and they can keep themselves busy with just a handful of flour or, better yet, a big ol' spoon and bowl so they can mix just like Mommy. It can get a little messy—and the scones might not look patisserie-perfect—but there's no yummier reward for a morning's work.

Scones are also great because they're such a versatile canvas for adding just about anything—dried or fresh fruit, chocolate, herbs, and even cheese! That's why I've included a plain base recipe, along with some of my favorite variations such as Blood Orange & Pistachio, Blueberry-Lemon, and Strawberry-Basil.

These scones are just the thing, whether they're piled high in a flour sack–lined basket for a serve-yourself breakfast buffet, arranged at each place setting for a polished sit-down brunch, or snapped up right from the baking sheet.

Makes 8 scones

BASE RECIPE:

2 cups all-purpose flour,
plus more for dusting

¼ cup sugar

6 tablespoons (¾ stick)
cold unsalted butter,
cut into ½-inch cubes

1 tablespoon baking powder

½ teaspoon kosher salt

½ cup whole milk

FLAVOR ADD-INS:
BLOOD ORANGE & PISTACHIO

2 tablespoons grated
blood orange zest

⅓ cup fresh blood orange juice
(from about 2 blood oranges)

Dash of pure vanilla extract

¾ cup chopped unsalted pistachios

BLUEBERRY-LEMON

¼ cup fresh lemon juice
(from about 1 lemon)

2 tablespoons grated lemon zest
(from about 2 lemons)

Dash of pure vanilla extract

1 cup fresh blueberries,
washed and dried

STRAWBERRY-BASIL

¼ cup fresh lemon juice
(from about 1 lemon)

2 tablespoons minced fresh basil

Dash of pure vanilla extract

1 cup fresh strawberries,
hulled and diced

Whipped Maple Butter
(page 46), for serving

Homemade Jam
(page 9), for serving

(Continued)

Preheat the oven to 400°F. Line a large baking sheet with parchment paper.

In the bowl of a stand mixer fitted with the paddle attachment, combine the flour, sugar, butter, baking powder, and salt. Beat on low speed until the dough reaches a sand-like consistency. Add the milk, increase the speed to medium, and mix just until the dough comes together; it may still be a bit crumbly. Use a spoon to gently fold in the ingredients from your variation of choice. If the variation includes fresh fruit, add this last because you don't want to mash it up too much.

Turn out the dough onto a floured surface and, using your hands, flatten the dough into a 12-inch-long, 6-inch-wide rectangle, about 1 inch thick. Divide the dough in half to form 2 squares. Cut an "X" across each square to create 4 triangular pieces, making 8 scones in total.

Place the scones 2 inches apart on the prepared baking sheet. Bake for 17 to 20 minutes, until golden brown. Let the scones cool on a wire rack for 5 minutes before serving.

Serve warm, with maple butter and jam.

HOMEMADE JAM

If there's one thing I find myself saying again and again, it's that nothing store-bought is ever going to be as tasty as homemade. I'm not suggesting that you have to start making every single item you can possibly cook from scratch, but by mastering a few staples, you can totally up your game. Jams are a great example of something that's super-easy to make and, once you learn the basics, can be an endless palette for all kinds of improvisation—throw in any fruit or combination of fruits and herbs. I love packaging them up in little jars and bringing them as host or hostess gifts, and it's a great project to do with kids. Just one word to the wise: Don't leave your jam unattended when it's cooking! Overcooked jam gets tacky and hard to spread. (Though it's still completely delicious.)

TOMATO JAM

Makes 2 cups

2 cups cherry tomatoes, stemmed (if necessary), washed, and dried

2 tablespoons fresh lemon juice (from about 1 lemon)

¾ cup sugar

2 teaspoons kosher salt

In a large saucepan, bring the tomatoes and lemon juice to a boil over medium-high heat. Cook, stirring and mashing continuously with a potato masher, for 1 minute. Stir in the sugar and salt and bring the mixture back to a boil. Cook, stirring continuously, until the mixture thickens slightly, begins to look syrupy, and coats the back of a spoon, 10 to 15 minutes. Be careful to not let the mixture get too thick, as it will thicken further while it cools. Remove the pot from the heat, transfer the jam to a heatproof jar, and let cool to room temperature, about 2 hours. Cover with a tight-fitting lid and refrigerate. It will keep for up to 2 weeks.

Raspberry Jam (p. 11)   Tomato Jam   Fig Jam (p. 11)

RASPBERRY JAM

Makes 2 cups

2 cups fresh raspberries
(about 12 ounces),
washed and dried

2 cups sugar

2 tablespoons fresh lemon juice
(from about 1 lemon)

In a large saucepan, bring the raspberries and lemon juice to a boil over medium-high heat. Cook, stirring and mashing continuously with a potato masher, for 1 minute. Stir in the sugar and bring the mixture to a boil once again. Cook, stirring continuously, until the mixture thickens slightly, begins to look syrupy, and coats the back of a spoon, 8 to 10 minutes. Be careful not to let the mixture get too thick, as it will thicken further while it cools. Remove the pot from the heat, transfer the jam to a heatproof jar, and let it cool to room temperature, about 2 hours. Cover with a tight-fitting lid and refrigerate. It will keep for up to 2 weeks.

FIG JAM

Makes 2 cups

2 cups black figs,
stemmed and quartered
(about 12 ounces)

2 cups sugar

1 teaspoon grated
lemon zest

2 tablespoons fresh lemon juice
(from about 1 lemon)

1 tablespoon
balsamic vinegar

In a large saucepan, combine the figs, sugar, lemon zest, and lemon juice and bring to a boil over medium-high heat. Cook, stirring and mashing continuously with a potato masher, for 15 minutes. Stir in the vinegar and cook for another 5 minutes, or until the jam is thick enough to coat the back of a spoon. Be careful not to let the mixture get too thick, as it will thicken further while it cools. Remove the pot from the heat, transfer the jam to a heatproof jar, and let it cool to room temperature, about 2 hours. Cover with a tight-fitting lid and refrigerate. It will keep for up to 2 weeks.

CHOCOLATE CHIP–BROWN BUTTER BANANA BREAD

I've had dozens of versions of banana bread over the years, but this one takes the (breakfast) cake. Greek yogurt and buttermilk give it dense creaminess while cinnamon, ginger, and chocolate chips make it decidedly un-boring. But the key ingredient is butter that's been browned until it's nutty and almost caramel in color and aroma. The result is a loaf that's light enough for breakfast but decadent enough for dessert.

Makes one 8-inch square loaf

4 tablespoons (½ stick) unsalted butter, plus more for greasing

1 cup whole wheat flour

1 cup almond flour

1 teaspoon baking soda

1 teaspoon ground cinnamon

1 teaspoon ground ginger

½ teaspoon kosher salt

¾ cup sugar

2 large eggs, beaten

⅓ cup plain whole-milk Greek yogurt

¼ cup buttermilk

1 teaspoon vanilla bean paste (see Note, page 223)

5 ripe bananas: 3 mashed and 2 thinly sliced lengthwise

½ cup semisweet chocolate chips

Preheat the oven to 350°F. Grease an 8-inch square baking pan with butter.

Melt the butter in a small sauté pan over medium heat. Swirl the pan to evenly distribute the butter on the bottom and heat until the foam disappears and the butter turns a light brown color, about 2 minutes, being careful not to let it burn. Pour the brown butter into a large bowl and set aside to cool.

In a separate large bowl, combine the flours, baking soda, cinnamon, ginger, and salt. Set aside.

Whisk the sugar, eggs, yogurt, buttermilk, and vanilla bean paste into the cooled brown butter. Use a spoon or spatula to stir in the mashed bananas, followed by the flour mixture. Fold in the chocolate chips.

Pour the batter into the prepared pan and top with the sliced bananas. Bake for 55 minutes to 1 hour, until a toothpick inserted into the middle comes out clean. Let the bread stand at room temperature for at least 15 minutes before slicing and serving.

CHIA SEED PUDDING

My romance with this super-simple dish started in Hawaii. I couldn't believe how rich and creamy it was—like super-decadent oatmeal. And my son can't get enough of it, which makes this mama very happy. Chia seeds are packed with nutrients, especially fiber and protein, so this is a particularly great breakfast for fueling you throughout the day. Plus, you make it ahead (the chia seeds need time to plump up), which means it can be all packed up and ready to grab in the morning. Or if you're having company, you can dress it up in pretty glasses or bowls. It's a great canvas for different flavors, and the toppings are endless—pretty much any fresh or dried fruit would look pretty and taste great. Toasted coconut and dried mango are my go-tos if I want to bring some sunny island vibes to my breakfast table.

Serves 2

1 cup unsweetened full-fat coconut milk

1 cup plain whole-milk Greek yogurt

2 tablespoons maple syrup

1 tablespoon vanilla bean paste (see Note, page 223)

¼ cup chia seeds

Toasted unsweetened shredded coconut, for garnish

Chopped dried mango, for garnish

In a medium bowl, whisk together the coconut milk, yogurt, maple syrup, and vanilla bean paste. Whisk in the chia seeds until combined. Cover and refrigerate overnight.

Sprinkle with toasted coconut and dried mango and serve.

POACHED EGG TOASTS WITH KALE

My husband has a chicken problem—and luckily, he's finally admitted it. It seems like everyone with a hen who needs a home knows that Brady can't say no, and that's how we ended up with eight (!) chickens living in our backyard. The girls give us six to eight eggs (or "butt nuggets," as Brady calls them) a day, which means we eat *a lot* of eggs. I'm always trying to come up with new ways to eat them, because one can only have so many frittatas.

People are always talking about 6-minute eggs, 9-minute eggs—and that's all fine and good—but my favorite, very unfussy egg preparation is poached. No immersion circulator, hot oil, or fancy flipping involved, just simmering water. And there's just nothing like that rich, golden yolk seeping into everything else on your plate. Or in this case, into toast that's been heaped with simply sautéed kale.

Serves 2

2 tablespoons
extra-virgin olive oil

2 cups Tuscan kale,
thick ribs removed, leaves
coarsely chopped or torn

Juice of ½ lemon

Kosher salt and freshly
ground black pepper

2 thick slices of bread of
your choice (I love sourdough
or multi-grain), toasted

1 tablespoon distilled
white vinegar

2 large eggs

¼ cup crumbled feta cheese,
for garnish

Smoked paprika, for garnish

In a medium sauté pan, heat the olive oil over medium-high heat. Add the kale and lemon juice and cook, stirring, until the greens are wilted, 2 to 3 minutes. Season with salt and pepper. Divide the kale between the slices of toast and set aside.

In a medium saucepan, bring 4 cups water plus the vinegar to a boil over medium-high heat. (There should be enough water in the pot to completely cover your eggs after you add them.) Reduce the heat to maintain a simmer. Crack each egg into a small bowl, one at a time, and then bring the bowl close to the surface of the simmering water and gently slip each egg into the water. (I sometimes use a spoon to help push the egg whites closer to the yolk to make a nice, round poached egg.) Cover the pot and turn off the heat. Let the eggs cook for 4 minutes, or until the whites are set but the yolks are still bright yellow and runny.

Use a slotted spoon to carefully remove the eggs from the water. Lightly tap the bottom of the spoon on a paper towel to remove excess water from the egg and place one egg on top of each toast. Garnish with crumbled feta and a pinch of smoked paprika.

BLOODY CAESAR WITH MAPLE-FENNEL BACON

I've always loved Bloody Marys, so when I went to Canada many, many (many) years ago, I was really intrigued by the Bloody Caesars I saw on menus there. I'd order them not knowing what they were, and they ended up being pretty much the best Bloody Marys I'd ever had. I finally asked what made them that much tastier and found out it was the addition of Clamato, a blend of tomato juice and clam juice. You'd never know there was any shellfish involved, though. It just lends a salty, briny flavor that softens the sweet acidity of the tomato juice. I had to come up with my own version, which I of course put over the top with a spear of Maple-Fennel Bacon. Because cheers to Canada! Also, who needs celery?!

Serves 6

8 cups Clamato juice

8 ounces vodka

Juice of 3 lemons

¼ cup prepared horseradish

1 tablespoon Worcestershire sauce

Freshly ground black pepper

Celery salt, for garnish

Ice

Maple-Fennel Bacon (recipe follows), for garnish

In a pitcher, combine the Clamato, vodka, lemon juice, horseradish, and Worcestershire. Stir well. Season with pepper and celery salt.

Spread a couple of tablespoons of celery salt on a plate. Dip the rims of six highball glasses in water and then press them into the salt to coat. Add ice to the glasses, then pour the Bloody Caesar over the ice and garnish each glass with Maple-Fennel Bacon.

MAPLE-FENNEL BACON

This is one of those insanely delicious things that you will make and your life will kind of never be the same again. I've always been a huge fan of the salty-sweet combination, and when you glaze bacon with maple and surprisingly sweet fennel, you get just that. It's the kind of bacon that anybody who eats bacon says is the best they've ever had.

Makes 12 slices

3 tablespoons maple syrup

1 tablespoon dark brown sugar

12 thick-cut bacon slices

2 teaspoons fennel seeds, crushed

Freshly ground black pepper

Preheat the oven to 375°F. Line a rimmed baking sheet with aluminum foil and set a wire rack inside.

In a small bowl, whisk together the maple syrup and brown sugar. Set aside.

Lay the bacon on the rack in a single layer, making sure that none of the slices are touching. Brush each slice with the syrup-sugar mixture and sprinkle with the crushed fennel seeds and a few cracks of black pepper.

Bake for 20 to 25 minutes, until the bacon is browned and crispy. Use a spatula to loosen the bacon from the rack so it doesn't stick as it cools. Let cool for 5 minutes before serving.

BREAKFAST NACHOS

This is a play on *chilaquiles*, a traditional Mexican breakfast dish that's essentially fried tortillas drenched with salsa and topped with refried beans and eggs. While there's absolutely nothing wrong with the original, I figured we could kick it up a notch by layering potato chips (because what's breakfast without potatoes?) with sausage, spiced Cuban-style black beans, scrambled eggs, and a Sriracha mayo drizzle. You could also skip the chips and roll up everything in a tortilla for breakfast burritos—just don't tell Brady, or you might have an extra guest at the breakfast table.

Serves 4

3 tablespoons extra-virgin olive oil

12 ounces breakfast sausages, casings removed

2 red bell peppers, diced

1 small yellow onion, diced

6 large eggs, beaten

½ cup mayonnaise

6 tablespoons Sriracha

Pinch of sugar

8 to 10 ounces large, sturdy potato chips, such as Kettle brand

½ cup Cuban-Style Black Beans (page 141)

¼ cup crumbled cotija cheese, for garnish

¼ cup fresh cilantro, for garnish (optional)

Coat the bottom of a large skillet with 1 tablespoon of the olive oil and heat the oil over medium-high heat. Add the sausage and cook, breaking it into small pieces with a spoon while it browns, for about 10 minutes. Using a slotted spoon, transfer the cooked sausage to a bowl, leaving any excess fat in the pan. Set aside.

Add the bell peppers and onion to the skillet and cook, stirring occasionally, until softened, about 5 minutes. Transfer the vegetables to the bowl with the sausage and toss. Set aside.

Coat the bottom of a clean nonstick skillet with the remaining 2 tablespoons olive oil and heat the oil over medium-high heat. Add the eggs and stir continuously with a spoon or spatula until they're fully cooked and fluffy, 5 to 6 minutes. Set aside.

In a small bowl, whisk together the mayonnaise, Sriracha, and sugar.

To assemble, arrange the potato chips on a platter and top with the sausage mixture, Cuban-Style Black Beans, scrambled eggs, and a drizzle of the Sriracha mayo. Sprinkle with the cotija cheese and cilantro, if desired, and serve.

GREEN EGGS 'N' STEAK FOR TWO

A greasy-spoon staple gets major polish when you pan-sear a bone-in rib-eye in a skillet, then throw in two eggs to cook over-easy (while sopping up all those lovely, meaty juices). And then there's the chimichurri, a super-bright, herbaceous sauce that makes the whole thing worthy of a breakfast date for two.

I love having a jar of chimichurri in the fridge because it's the perfect finishing touch for so many things—on any kind of meat coming off the grill, fish, shrimp, roasted veggies, you name it. And you can add a splash more vinegar to turn it into a salad dressing. Luckily, you'll have leftovers from this recipe, so stash 'em in the fridge for up to a week and see what fun new dishes you can come up with!

Serves 2

FOR THE CHIMICHURRI:

¼ cup chopped fresh
flat-leaf parsley

¼ cup chopped fresh oregano

4 sprigs fresh mint

2 garlic cloves, minced

¼ cup extra-virgin olive oil

Juice of ½ lime

Kosher salt and
freshly ground black pepper

Pinch of red pepper flakes

FOR THE STEAK AND EGGS:

1 (6-ounce) bone-in rib-eye
or sirloin steak

Kosher salt and freshly ground
black pepper

2 tablespoons unsalted butter,
plus more as needed

2 large eggs

For the chimichurri: Combine all the ingredients in a medium bowl and stir to fully incorporate. Set aside.

For the steak and eggs: Season the steak with salt and pepper.

In a large cast-iron skillet, melt the butter over medium-high heat. Place the steak on one side of the skillet, leaving room for the eggs. Cook until the steak has a dark brown sear, 3 to 4 minutes per side for medium-rare. If the pan gets dry, add another tablespoon of butter. Reduce the heat to medium-low and add the eggs. Season with a pinch of salt and pepper. When the whites start to set, cover the skillet with a lid and cook for 2 to 3 minutes more.

Serve with the Chimichurri Sauce.

Egg Whites, Sweet Potato Hash
Browns & Mango Guacamole (p. 28)

EGG WHITES, SWEET POTATO HASH BROWNS & MANGO GUACAMOLE

I fell in love with a version of this dish at a restaurant when I was living in New York, and pretty much went back constantly to eat it again and again. I just couldn't get enough of all the textures and flavors layered together—the thin, crispy sweet potatoes; fluffy egg whites; and a dollop of guacamole, made just the tiniest bit sweeter with bits of fresh mango and orange juice instead of lime. Somehow it managed to be filling and light at the same time. Now I make my own version, especially because it's pretty healthy, which means I can have seconds!

Serves 4 to 6

FOR THE MANGO GUACAMOLE:

3 ripe medium avocados, pitted and peeled

½ small red onion, finely chopped

½ large jalapeño, seeded and minced

1 cup chopped fresh cilantro leaves

¼ cup crumbled cotija cheese, plus more for garnish

3 tablespoons fresh lime juice (from about 2 limes)

1 teaspoon kosher salt

½ teaspoon chili powder

1 cup diced mango

FOR THE SWEET POTATO HASH BROWNS:

1½ pounds sweet potatoes, peeled

1 medium shallot

2 large eggs, lightly beaten

2 tablespoons all-purpose flour, plus more as needed

1 teaspoon kosher salt

1 teaspoon freshly ground black pepper

2 to 4 tablespoons vegetable oil

3 tablespoons unsalted butter

FOR THE EGG WHITES:

12 large eggs, at room temperature

¼ cup heavy cream

3 tablespoons extra-virgin olive oil

Kosher salt and freshly ground black pepper

For the mango guacamole: In a medium bowl, mash the avocados with a potato masher or the back of a fork. I like leaving mine a little chunky, but feel free to make yours completely smooth. Stir in the red onion, jalapeño, cilantro, cotija cheese, lime juice, salt, and chili powder. Gently fold in the mango. Refrigerate with plastic wrap pressed directly against the surface until ready to serve.

For the sweet potato hash browns: Preheat the oven to 200°F.

Working over a clean kitchen towel, grate the sweet potatoes and shallots on the large holes of a box grater. Gather up the edges of the towel and wring out the excess water over the sink. Put the sweet potato mixture in a large bowl and stir in the eggs, flour, salt, and pepper. If the mixture is still very wet and loose, add more flour 1 tablespoon at a time until the batter comes together.

In a griddle or large skillet, heat 1 tablespoon of the vegetable oil and 1 tablespoon of the butter over medium heat. Working in batches, add 2 tablespoons of the potato mixture in a small mound on the griddle and gently press down to form a patty. Cook until golden brown, 3 to 4 minutes. Flip and cook for another 4 minutes, or until the second side is also golden brown and crisp. Transfer to a wire rack set over a large baking sheet. Repeat with the remaining potato mixture, adding more vegetable oil and butter when the pan gets dry. Transfer the hash browns to the oven to keep warm while you assemble the rest of the dish.

For the egg whites: Separate the eggs, collecting the whites in a large bowl. (And don't just toss out the yolks—you can store them in the fridge for up to 3 days and use them for egg wash or ice cream, or even cook them up for your dogs.) Whisk the egg whites for about 20 seconds while slowly streaming in the heavy cream.

In a nonstick saucepan, heat the olive oil over medium heat. Pour the egg whites into the pan and cook, using a spoon or spatula to gently scramble the eggs and break them up into large pieces, until they are set, 2 to 3 minutes. Cook for another 2 minutes, then remove the pan from the heat. Season with salt and pepper.

To assemble: Place a hash brown patty on each plate. Top evenly with the egg whites and finish with a dollop of the guacamole.

EGG & SAUSAGE CASSEROLE

There's no greater dish for feeding a crowd or just to have ready to go in the morning for your own troops. It's essentially savory bread pudding that's loaded with all your favorite breakfast components: bacon, sausage, and eggs. Oh yeah! Plus, I throw in a whole mess of veggies, so this is a great solution for cleaning out the crisper. Assemble it the night before in a pretty oven-to-table casserole dish, bake it off in the morning, sprinkle it with feta cheese, and put it right on the table.

Serves 4 to 6

2 tablespoons extra-virgin olive oil, plus more for greasing

1½ cups cubed country loaf bread (1-inch cubes)

½ pound sweet Italian sausage, casings removed

1 medium yellow onion, finely chopped

1 (10-ounce) package fresh spinach leaves

⅓ cup chopped drained oil-packed sun-dried tomatoes

Kosher salt and freshly ground black pepper

10 large eggs

½ cup whole milk

¼ cup crumbled feta cheese

Preheat the oven to 400°F. Grease a 9-by-13-inch baking dish with olive oil.

Gently toss the cubed bread with 1 tablespoon of the olive oil and spread it over a large baking sheet in a single layer. Bake for about 10 minutes, until toasted and golden brown. Set aside.

In a medium sauté pan, heat the remaining 1 tablespoon olive oil over medium-high heat. Add the sausage and onion and cook, breaking up the sausage into small pieces with a wooden spoon, until the sausage is cooked through and the onion is translucent, 8 to 10 minutes. Stir in the spinach and cook until wilted, 2 to 3 minutes. Add the sun-dried tomatoes and cook for an additional 2 minutes. Season with salt and pepper. Set aside.

In a medium bowl, beat together the eggs, milk, ¼ teaspoon salt, and ¼ teaspoon pepper until frothy, about 1 minute.

Spread the toasted bread cubes in a single layer over the bottom of the prepared baking dish. Layer the sausage-and-vegetable mixture over the top of the bread cubes, then pour in the egg mixture so it covers the entire casserole. Refrigerate overnight or for at least 4 hours.

When ready to serve, preheat the oven to 350°F.

Remove the casserole from the fridge and sprinkle with the feta cheese. Bake for 1 hour, or until set. Let cool for 10 to 15 minutes before serving.

THE BEG
(BACON-EGG-GRIDDLE SANDWICH)

Brady requests this at least once a week, if he's not asking for burritos. And that's fine by me, because it's another great way to use up all those lovely eggs coming from our gals in the backyard (see page 17 for more on the ladies). It's your classic griddle sandwich—sourdough bread heaped with sour cream scrambled eggs, applewood-smoked bacon, and cheddar cheese. Easily made, easily appreciated, and easily demolished.

Serves 2

4 slices applewood-smoked bacon

6 large eggs, at room temperature

2 tablespoons sour cream
or heavy cream

2 tablespoons unsalted butter

Kosher salt and freshly ground
black pepper

4 thick slices good-quality
sourdough bread

8 slices cheddar cheese

In a large skillet, cook the bacon over medium heat until the fat has rendered and both sides are crispy and golden brown, 6 to 8 minutes. Transfer the bacon to a paper towel–lined plate. Do not wipe out the pan! Set aside. (At this point I excuse everyone from the kitchen so I don't have to guard the bacon while I finish making everything else.)

In a medium bowl, whisk together the eggs and sour cream.

In a nonstick skillet, melt 1 tablespoon of the butter over medium heat. Pour the egg mixture into the pan and cook, using a spoon or spatula to gently scramble the eggs and break them up into large pieces, until the eggs are set, 2 to 3 minutes. Cook for another 2 minutes, then remove the pan from the heat. Season with salt and pepper.

Top each slice of bread with 2 slices of cheese. Layer each sandwich with 2 strips of bacon and half the eggs. Top each sandwich with a second slice of bread.

In the skillet you used for the bacon, melt the remaining 1 tablespoon butter over medium heat. Add the sandwiches. Cover the pan and cook for 3 minutes. Flip the sandwiches, cover the pan again, and cook until the cheese has completely melted and the bread is toasted and golden, another 2 to 3 minutes. Get started on a second batch, because these go quick!

CHERRY & MAPLE GRANOLA

Granola definitely falls into the "homemade kicks store-bought butt" category. Not only will it taste fresher and more vibrant than anything that's been sitting around in a box on a shelf, but you can take the basic idea and customize it with any mix-ins you want. I particularly love this combo of richly sweet maple and tart dried cherries. Keep a batch in an airtight container in your pantry and you'll always have a handy breakfast (just add yogurt or milk), a great topping for muffins or ice cream, or a sweet favor guests take home and eat the morning after you've had them over for a party. The only problem is that they'll keep coming back for more, because it truly is the best granola anyone has ever had.

Serves 4

3 cups old-fashioned oats

1 cup coarsely chopped raw unsalted almonds

1 cup coarsely chopped raw unsalted cashews

2 tablespoons chia seeds

2 tablespoons ground cinnamon

¼ teaspoon sea salt

½ cup maple syrup

½ cup coconut oil, melted

1 teaspoon pure vanilla extract

1 cup dried cherries

½ cup unsweetened shredded coconut

Preheat the oven to 300°F. Line a large rimmed baking sheet with parchment paper.

In a large bowl, thoroughly combine the oats, almonds, cashews, chia seeds, cinnamon, and salt. In a separate medium bowl, combine the maple syrup, melted coconut oil, and vanilla. Add the wet ingredients to the dry mixture and combine using a wooden spoon. Stir in the dried cherries and shredded coconut, making sure the ingredients are well combined.

Spread the mixture over the prepared baking sheet in a single layer. Bake, turning the granola with a spatula every 8 to 10 minutes, for about 35 minutes, until the granola is golden brown and your kitchen smells of warm cinnamon and toasted coconut. (Who needs a candle?!) Remove the granola from the oven and let it cool before serving or storing. Store in an airtight container for up to 1 month.

PEANUT BUTTER & BANANA–STUFFED FRENCH TOAST WITH NUTELLA DRIZZLE

It doesn't get much more decadent than two egg-dredged slices of soft, sweet challah stuffed with peanut butter and banana slices, toasted up in butter, then slathered with caramelized brown butter bananas and finished off with a Nutella drizzle. Hungry yet?

Serves 4

¾ cup whole milk

½ cup Nutella

6 large eggs,
at room temperature

2 tablespoons sugar

1 teaspoon vanilla bean paste
(see Note, page 223)

8 (½-inch-thick) slices brioche

½ cup smooth peanut butter

4 ripe bananas, sliced

2 tablespoons unsalted butter

½ cup pecans, coarsely chopped
(see Note)

In a medium saucepan, heat ¼ cup of the milk over medium heat until just bubbling around the edges of the pan, 1 to 2 minutes (do not boil). Whisk in 1 to 2 tablespoons of the Nutella (it will be rather watery). Add another 2 tablespoons of the Nutella and whisk. The mixture will thicken and some lumps may form. Whisk until smooth. Continue adding the remaining Nutella 1 tablespoon at a time, whisking thoroughly after each addition, until all of the Nutella is fully incorporated and you have a smooth sauce. Set aside to cool to room temperature.

In a shallow medium bowl, whisk together the remaining ½ cup milk, the eggs, sugar, and vanilla bean paste. Set aside.

Spread each brioche slice with 1 tablespoon of the peanut butter. Arrange the banana slices in a single layer on 4 of the brioche slices. Top with the remaining brioche slices, peanut butter–side down.

Place a sandwich in the egg mixture and let it sit until the bread is soaked through, about 1 minute per side. Repeat with the remaining sandwiches.

Melt the butter on a griddle or in a large skillet over medium heat. Cook the sandwiches in batches, so as not to overcrowd the pan, until the bread is golden and firm, 1 to 2 minutes per side.

To serve, drizzle each sandwich with the Nutella sauce and top with a sprinkle of chopped pecans.

Note: To toast just about any nut or seed, simply spread them in a single layer in a dry skillet and gently toast over medium-low heat until the nuts are fragrant and lightly browned, 1 to 2 minutes. Give them a stir or a toss every so often so they toast evenly, and watch for any sign of burning. Remove from the pan to cool.

RASPBERRY TOASTER TARTS

A piping-hot homemade Pop-Tart? Oozing with that signature neon-red filling and glazed just like the original? You heard that right, folks! And believe me, they couldn't be simpler to make. You can package 'em up in little waxed paper sandwich pockets and send them with your kids as they run out the door in the morning, or put them out as a fun brunch starter.

Feel free to tailor the filling to whatever fruit is in season or whatever fruit you like. You can always use canned fruit if you can't swing fresh—it doesn't take away from the fact that you made something from scratch.

Makes 6 toaster tarts

FOR THE CRUST:

2½ cups all-purpose flour

1 tablespoon granulated sugar

¾ teaspoon kosher salt

1 cup (2 sticks) cold unsalted butter, cut into ½-inch cubes

¼ to ½ cup ice water

FOR THE FILLING:

4 cups fresh raspberries (about 1 pound), washed and dried

½ cup maple syrup

Juice of ½ lemon

½ teaspoon ground cinnamon

Pinch of kosher salt

3 tablespoons plus 1 teaspoon tapioca flour

2 tablespoons cold unsalted butter, cut into ½-inch cubes

1 large egg white

FOR THE ICING:

1 cup powdered sugar, sifted

¼ teaspoon pure vanilla extract

Turbinado sugar, for serving

For the crust: In a food processor fitted with the pastry blade, combine the flour, granulated sugar, and salt and pulse a few times to combine. Add the butter and pulse again, until the mixture resembles fine gravel. Add the ice water a few tablespoons at a time and pulse until the dough comes together and forms a ball. Remove the dough from the food processor and divide it in half. Shape each piece into a disk and wrap in plastic. Refrigerate for at least 30 minutes.

For the filling: In a large bowl, combine the berries, maple syrup, lemon juice, cinnamon, and salt. Add the tapioca flour and butter and stir to combine. Set aside.

To assemble: Preheat the oven to 425°F. Line a large baking sheet with parchment paper.

In a small bowl, whisk together the egg white and 1 tablespoon water to make an egg wash. Set aside.

Remove the dough disks from the refrigerator. Let them come to room temperature for about 10 minutes.

On a lightly floured work surface, roll out 1 disk of dough into an ⅛-inch-thick rectangle, 10 inches wide and 15 inches long. Use a sharp knife to trim the edges and cut the dough into three 10-by-4-inch rectangles.

(Continued)

Working with one pastry rectangle at a time, brush the edges with the egg wash and heap 3 to 4 tablespoons of the filling into the center of the rectangle, leaving a 1-inch margin of pastry around the filling. Fold the dough over the filling so that the short ends of the rectangle meet, forming a 5-by-4-inch pocket. Press the top edges into the bottom edges to seal. Crimp the 3 sealed edges with the tines of a fork. Using a sharp knife, cut a few slits in the top to vent. Brush with the egg wash and transfer to the prepared baking sheet. Repeat with the other 2 pastry rectangles before repeating the entire filling process with the second disk of dough.

Bake the tarts for 10 minutes, then reduce the oven temperature to 350°F. Bake until the crust is golden brown and the filling is bubbling, about 15 minutes. Transfer the tarts to a wire rack and let them cool completely.

For the icing: In a small bowl, combine the powdered sugar, vanilla, and 1½ tablespoons water. Evenly coat each cooled tart with a spoonful of the icing. Sprinkle with the turbinado sugar and let the icing set for about 30 minutes before serving. Freeze any leftover tarts in a sealed plastic bag and warm in the oven or in the toaster on low heat when ready to serve.

YOGURT PANCAKES WITH WHIPPED MAPLE BUTTER

There are two kinds of breakfasts in my house: There's the pretty standard scenario where it's all you can do to get *something* edible on the table for the family. And then there are those magical mornings when the stars align, and you find yourself with just enough time to pull together a meal that's a little more special than cereal.

Luckily, these pancakes fit the bill for both occasions. The batter takes minutes to whip up, and everyone can dress their own stacks with whatever you have on hand. Fresh berries are a big hit with Harper and Holt, while Brady and I are partial to caramelized bananas and spicy maple syrup. And nothing is more impressive to a brunch crowd than a batch of these babies piled high on a cake platter with layers of Whipped Maple Butter—and maybe, just maybe, fresh whipped cream—in between.

I've been making my pancakes with yogurt instead of traditional buttermilk for as long as I can remember. It gives these hotcakes a creamier, more luscious consistency, but still with that classic tang and perfectly fluffy texture.

Serves 4

1 cup all-purpose flour

½ cup almond flour

2 tablespoons sugar

2 teaspoons baking powder

½ teaspoon kosher salt

2 large eggs, at room temperature

¾ cup plain whole-milk
Greek yogurt

2 tablespoons vegetable oil

1 teaspoon pure vanilla extract

¾ cup whole milk

Unsalted butter, for greasing

Whipped Maple Butter
(recipe follows), for serving

TOPPING SUGGESTIONS:

Chopped nuts

Fresh fruit

Dried fruit

Raspberry or Fig Jam (page 11)
or store-bought jam

Toasted unsweetened coconut

(Continued)

In a medium bowl, whisk together the flours, sugar, baking powder, and salt. In a separate small bowl, combine the eggs, yogurt, oil, and vanilla. Add the wet ingredients to the dry and mix well. Stir in the milk, being careful not to overmix—some lumps are okay.

Heat a griddle or large skillet over medium heat.

Add ½ tablespoon of the butter to the griddle. When it starts to foam, pour ⅓ cup of the batter per pancake onto the hot griddle. Cook until the batter starts to bubble, about 2 minutes. Use a metal spatula to flip the pancakes over and cook for 1 minute more. Transfer the pancakes to a large plate. Cover the plate with a clean kitchen towel to keep the pancakes warm. Repeat until all the batter has been used.

Serve the pancakes with a dollop of the Whipped Maple Butter and your favorite toppings.

WHIPPED MAPLE BUTTER

One of my go-to so-fancy-but-so-easy tricks is making flavored butters. The basic formula is melting down unsalted butter, adding your ingredients of choice—whether sweet or savory—then chilling it down again. This maple version is a clear winner for slathering on biscuits, scones, cornbread, waffles, and pancakes.

Makes about 1 cup

¾ cup (1½ sticks) cold unsalted butter, cut into ½-inch cubes

⅓ cup maple syrup

Put the butter in a medium saucepan over high heat. Cook, stirring, until the butter is melted, foamy, and golden brown, 4 to 5 minutes. Stir in the maple syrup and cook for 1 minute more. Remove the pot from the heat and transfer the butter to a heatproof bowl. Cover with plastic wrap and refrigerate for about 30 minutes, until the butter is firm but still soft enough to stir. Whip the butter with a whisk until smooth and creamy, about 1 minute. Serve immediately or store in the fridge in an airtight container for up to 2 weeks.

LUNCHING
AND
MIDDAY
MUNCHING

Breakfast and dinner have their moments, but lunch is pretty special in my book. It's a much-needed afternoon break, a time when you can just sit and nourish yourself and take a nice, long (sort of), deep breath. I love feeding people lunch because it's a meal that so often gets rushed through or overlooked. Plus, how many turkey sandwiches or sad salads can you eat?! I like to keep this meal on the lighter side—so you don't feel like you need a siesta afterward—and offer refreshing updates on the standbys, like Creamy Sweet Corn Soup, Quinoa Salad with Currants and Pecans, and Rustic Turkey Panini with Brie, Apples & Watercress (how's

that for a turkey revamp?!). If it's during the week, I'll either host a quick grab 'n' go power lunch for a chance to catch up with friends before we all run back to work, or I'll pack up a few things for me, Brady, and the kids to take with us when we all scatter our separate ways. Simple sandwiches become a nice treat in sweet waxed-paper-and-twine packages, while soups and salads look extra-scrumptious packed in jars (just don't forget to leave the dressing on the side or you'll end up with soggy lettuce!). Of course, things get a whole lot more relaxed on the weekends when you can all just sit and graze, but either way, lunch is an opportunity to reboot and restore, then face the rest of the day.

CREAMY SWEET CORN SOUP

There's nothing that says summer like fresh sweet corn. It reminds me of being a kid and having lunch outside, still wearing my bathing suit after running around in the sprinklers all morning. Now my own kids get to sit in the yard—swimsuits and all—with a huge ear of corn that's hot off the grill.

While there's nothing wrong with keeping things simple and on the cob, one of the most indulgent ways to enjoy corn is adding all that pretty yellow sweetness to a creamy chowder. It's a snap to make ahead (perfect for the pre-party checklist!), can be served hot or cold, and goes with all kinds of garnishes. Try going spicy (throw a little jalapeño on top), sweet (drizzle with herb-infused honey), meaty (bacon!), cheesy (a sprinkle of feta), or nutty (a handful of chopped pecans).

Serves 4

6 ears yellow corn

1 to 3 cups chicken broth

2 tablespoons unsalted butter

1 medium yellow onion,
thinly sliced

1 medium russet potato,
peeled and grated

Kosher salt

½ cup heavy cream

Freshly ground black pepper

3 tablespoons chopped fresh
chives, for garnish

Extra-virgin olive oil,
for garnish

Use a sharp knife to cut the kernels off the ears of corn. Set the kernels aside in a medium bowl. Place the cobs in a large pot and add just enough water to cover them. Put the pot over medium-high heat and bring to a boil. Reduce the heat to medium-low and cook for 30 minutes. Remove and discard the cobs. Measure the remaining liquid and add enough broth to make 5 cups total liquid.

Melt the butter in the same pot over medium heat. Add the onion and grated potato and cook, stirring, until the onion is soft and translucent, about 5 minutes. Add the liquid, 6 cups of the corn kernels, and 1 teaspoon salt. Partially cover the pot with a lid and bring to a boil. Reduce the heat to medium-low and simmer for 20 minutes. Remove from the heat and let cool for 15 to 20 minutes.

Working in batches, puree the soup in a blender on high speed, 2 to 3 minutes per batch.

Bring ½ cup water to a boil in a small pot. Add the remaining corn kernels (there should be about ¾ cup) and cook until tender, about 7 minutes. Drain and reserve.

Return the pureed soup to the stockpot over medium heat. Add the reserved cooked corn kernels and cook until warmed through, 10 minutes. Stir in the cream and season with salt and pepper.

Garnish with the chives and a drizzle of olive oil and serve.

SPRING PEA SOUP

Peas are one of my favorite veggies—they're light, sweet, and crisp, and they're a telltale sign that spring is here. Luckily, we grow peas in our garden, so I always have my fair share to play around with in the kitchen. When I'm not just snacking on them straight up, I love pureeing them into a simple soup that's fragrant with shallots, garlic, and mint (the ultimate in springtime freshness!); then I sneak in a handful of spinach for an extra dose of green.

Serves 2 or 3

1 tablespoon coconut oil

3 large shallots, sliced (about ½ cup)

2 garlic cloves, minced

1 pound fresh sweet peas, shelled (or use frozen)

1½ tablespoons chopped fresh mint

Kosher salt and freshly ground black pepper

15 baby spinach leaves

Crème fraîche, for serving

Melt the coconut oil in a large stockpot over medium heat. Add the shallots and garlic and cook, stirring, until the shallots are tender, 4 to 5 minutes. Add 3½ cups water and bring to a boil. Reduce the heat to medium-low and simmer for 30 minutes. Add the peas, mint, 2 teaspoons salt, and a pinch of pepper and bring back to a boil. Reduce the heat to medium-low and simmer for 5 minutes. Remove from the heat and let cool to room temperature.

Puree the soup in a blender until very smooth (be careful when blending hot liquids). Add the spinach leaves and blend again until completely smooth. Season with salt and pepper.

Serve each bowl with a dollop (about 1 tablespoon) of crème fraîche.

CHICKEN TORTILLA SOUP

This is my take on the traditional Mexican soup, a tomato-based broth that's made super aromatic by garlic and onions, plus a little heat from jalapeños. It's hearty enough to fill you up, but it's not going to bog you down for the rest of the day. This soup is simple enough for a weekday meal, but it's also a fun dish to entertain with because you can set out a big spread of toppings such as chopped onion and scallions, sliced radishes and jicama, Homemade Tortilla Chips (page 201)—or store-bought—guacamole or sliced avocado, a variety of grated cheese—you get the idea! It's especially perfect as a lighter option when having people over to watch a big game on TV. If you are going to be serving this for a crowd, you can leave out the chicken and use veggie broth instead to make this vegetarian-friendly. Then add shredded chicken (or short ribs or pulled pork) to your toppings bonanza for the meat eaters.

Serves 4

2 tablespoons extra-virgin olive oil

1 cup finely chopped scallions

2 jalapeños, seeded and minced

2 garlic cloves, minced

3 cups chicken broth

2 Roma (plum) tomatoes, seeded and diced

½ teaspoon ground cumin

½ teaspoon ground coriander

¼ teaspoon chili powder

Kosher salt and freshly ground black pepper

1 pound skinless, boneless chicken breasts (about 2 medium breasts)

3 tablespoons fresh lime juice (from about 2 limes)

2 tablespoons coarsely chopped fresh cilantro

Sliced avocado, for serving

Homemade Tortilla Chips (page 201), for serving

Cotija cheese, for serving

In a large pot, heat the olive oil over medium heat. Add the scallions and jalapeños and cook, stirring, until tender, about 2 minutes. Add the garlic and cook, stirring, until slightly fragrant, 1 minute. Stir in the broth, tomatoes, cumin, coriander, and chili powder and season with salt and pepper. Add the chicken breasts, raise the heat to medium-high, and bring the mixture to a boil. Reduce the heat to medium and cover with a lid. Cook until the chicken is completely cooked through, 10 to 15 minutes. Reduce the heat to maintain a simmer and remove the chicken breasts from the pot. Set aside to rest and cool slightly.

When cool enough to handle, shred the chicken and return it to the pot. Add the lime juice and cilantro.

Serve with sliced avocados, tortilla chips, and cotija, or any other toppings of your choice.

CUCUMBER GAZPACHO WITH WATERMELON & MINT

Gazpacho is traditionally made with tomatoes, but I got the idea to do a version with another summertime staple: cucumbers. I tossed in some creamy Greek yogurt for body, some watermelon for a little sweetness, fresh ginger and mint for brightness, and cayenne for just a little kick. The result? A refreshing take on a classic that's now my steamy-weather tonic. If I'm going to be at the grill all afternoon—or it's just too darn hot to turn on the stove—I love knowing this surprisingly rich and satisfying soup is only a blender spin away.

Cucumber Gazpacho can go with pretty much anything. Pair it with fish, seafood, chicken, or steak for a quick weeknight meal; put out a big batch at your next lobster boil; or set out dainty bowls for a girls' day in. It's a cinch to dress up gazpacho all ladylike, too: just sprinkle with toasted pepitas and feta, dot with fresh mint, and drizzle the whole lot with infused chili oil, which you can find in most specialty markets and some grocery stores.

Serves 4

4 large English cucumbers, peeled and chopped

2¼ cups diced seedless watermelon

1 cup plain whole-milk Greek yogurt

½ small sweet onion, thinly sliced

3 tablespoons fresh lemon juice (from about 2 lemons)

1 bunch fresh mint, leaves chopped

2 tablespoons chopped fresh cilantro

2 teaspoons kosher salt, plus more to taste

1 teaspoon grated fresh ginger

½ teaspoon cayenne pepper

½ cup pepitas (pumpkin seeds), toasted (see Note, page 38)

Crumbled feta cheese, for garnish

Chili oil, for garnish

In a large bowl, combine the cucumber, 2 cups of the watermelon, the yogurt, onion, lemon juice, all but 2 tablespoons of the mint, the cilantro, salt, ginger, and cayenne. Blend the mixture in small batches until smooth, transferring each batch to a pitcher or large bowl as you go. Cover and refrigerate for 2 hours.

Season with salt before serving. Divide the soup among chilled bowls and top with the remaining mint, remaining diced watermelon, the pepitas, feta, and a drizzle of chili oil.

QUINOA SALAD WITH CURRANTS & PECANS

I say quinoa salad is the new pasta salad! Just like pasta, it goes with just about any toppings and is delicious when tossed with a simple, light dressing—but it's also a great high-protein starch that doesn't land with a *thud* in your belly. This sweet-savory mix with red onions, currants, and pecans plus fresh Persian cucumbers and olive oil–lemon juice dressing is perfect as a side, or you could serve it on a bed of greens or with a cup of soup and call it lunch. It's perfect for packing up to go because it holds really nicely in the fridge, even overnight.

Serves 2 or 3

1 pound tricolor quinoa, cooked according to the package directions

½ small red onion, diced

½ cup dried currants

½ cup pecans, toasted (see Note, page 38)

½ cup diced Persian cucumber

¼ cup fresh lemon juice (from about 2 lemons)

¼ cup extra-virgin olive oil

Kosher salt and freshly ground black pepper

¼ cup crumbled feta cheese

1 tablespoon coarsely chopped fresh parsley

In a medium bowl, combine the cooked quinoa, onion, currants, pecans, and cucumber. Put the lemon juice in a separate small bowl and slowly whisk in the olive oil. Season with salt and pepper. Drizzle the dressing over the quinoa salad and toss to evenly coat. Top with the feta and parsley and serve.

TUNA STICKY RICE BOWL

It's no wonder people are all buzzing about *poke*, a Hawaiian surf-shack fixture that's usually a combo of sliced raw fish, fresh and pickled veggies, and tangy dressing on a bed of sticky rice. It's super refreshing and filling without being heavy. There are endless combinations of fish and veggie toppings you could make this with—or as I like to say, there's no wrong way to *poke*—but I like to load mine up with marinated tuna, avocado, and a pretty rainbow of sliced veggies like radishes, cucumbers, and heirloom carrots, which you can find at the farmers' market or even some grocery stores in beautiful colors like pastel yellow or deep purple. Then I drizzle it all with spicy mayo. Half the fun is decorating the bowl with your ingredients like a work of art. Who said you can't play with your food? Not me!

Serves 4

FOR THE TUNA-AVOCADO POKE:

1 pound sashimi-grade tuna, cut into ½-inch cubes

1 medium shallot, minced

¼ cup soy sauce

2 tablespoons untoasted sesame oil

2 teaspoons grated fresh ginger

1 jalapeño, seeded and minced (optional)

1 avocado, cut into ¼-inch slices

Kosher salt and freshly ground black pepper

FOR THE SPICY MAYO:

½ cup mayonnaise

2 teaspoons Sriracha

TO ASSEMBLE:

4 large Bibb lettuce leaves

4 cups cooked sushi rice

1 cup shelled fresh or frozen edamame

3 medium radishes, thinly sliced

1 Persian cucumber, thinly sliced

2 medium carrots, thinly sliced on an angle

2 tablespoons chopped macadamia nuts, toasted (see Note, page 38)

1 tablespoon black sesame seeds

For the tuna-avocado poke: In a medium bowl, combine the tuna, shallot, soy sauce, sesame oil, ginger, and jalapeño. Toss gently to combine. Cover and refrigerate for 1 to 2 hours. Just before serving, fold in the avocado and season with salt and pepper.

For the spicy mayo: In a medium bowl, whisk together the mayonnaise and Sriracha. Set aside.

To assemble: Place a lettuce leaf at the bottom of each serving bowl and mound 1 cup of the sushi rice on top. Pile a quarter of the tuna-avocado mixture on one side of each bowl and arrange the remaining ingredients on the other side in a decorative way, dividing the toppings evenly among the four bowls. Get creative!

SOUTHERN CALI SALAD WITH FARRO

This salad is all about Southern California—it's fresh, it's light, and it's got just the right healthy-to-delicious ratio. There's hearty, chewy farro plus tons of texture from jicama, Marcona almonds, grapes, and raisins. The whole lot gets heaped onto a big bed of greens—any kind will do—dotted with tangy goat cheese and drizzled with thyme vinaigrette. This is a great salad to make the day after you've cooked up a big batch of grains as a new spin on your leftovers, or toss in some roast chicken or anything else that came off the grill.

Serves 2

3 cups shredded Tuscan kale leaves, romaine lettuce, or arugula, washed and dried

½ cup cooked farro, rice, quinoa, or wheat berries

⅓ cup thinly sliced jicama

12 red or green grapes, thinly sliced

¼ cup golden raisins

¼ cup Marcona almonds

¼ cup balsamic vinegar

¾ teaspoon kosher salt, plus more to taste

½ teaspoon dried thyme

¼ teaspoon freshly ground black pepper, plus more to taste

¾ cup extra-virgin olive oil

4 ounces goat cheese, crumbled

In a large bowl, toss together the kale, farro, jicama, grapes, raisins, and almonds. In a separate medium bowl, whisk together the vinegar, salt, thyme, and pepper. Slowly stream in the olive oil as you whisk. Drizzle the dressing over the salad and toss to coat. Top with the goat cheese and season with salt and pepper.

NECTARINE CAPRESE SALAD

While I love a traditional caprese—the classic combination of tomatoes, mozzarella, and basil—you know I can't resist adding my own twist. When stone fruit season rolls around at the peak of summer, I throw some nectarines into the mix. They make a gorgeous couple with juicy, sweet heirloom tomatoes, which I then pair with burrata, mozzarella's more decadent cousin. It's a little pouch of fresh mozzarella that's filled with cheese curds and cream. When you slice into it, the cheese runs over the salad and mixes with the champagne vinaigrette to give everything a big dose of rich deliciousness. I like to do it tableside—it's a crowd-pleaser!

Serves 4

1 tablespoon champagne vinegar

1 teaspoon white balsamic vinegar

Kosher salt

3 tablespoons extra-virgin olive oil

1½ pounds heirloom tomatoes, cut into wedges

3 ripe nectarines, pitted and cut into wedges

8 ounces burrata cheese

¼ cup fresh basil leaves, torn

10 fresh mint leaves, thinly sliced

Freshly ground black pepper

Flaky sea salt, for serving

In a small bowl, whisk together the vinegars and a pinch of kosher salt. Continue to whisk as you slowly stream in the olive oil. Taste and adjust the seasoning if necessary. Set aside.

Arrange the tomato and nectarine wedges in an alternating pattern on a serving platter. Place the burrata on top and sprinkle with the basil and mint. Drizzle everything with the vinaigrette and finish with some pepper and a pinch of flaky sea salt. Serve immediately.

CHOPPED SALAD WITH CREAMY WASABI DRESSING

This variation of a (slightly heavier) lunch standby takes light-but-mighty powerhouses—almonds, edamame, and avocado—and pairs them with earthy roasted beets and a zesty, creamy wasabi dressing, which is pretty much the star of the show.

Serves 2

8 medium red or golden beets

Extra-virgin olive oil

Kosher salt

1 romaine heart, finely chopped

½ head iceberg lettuce, finely chopped

1½ cups shelled fresh or frozen edamame

4 Persian cucumbers, peeled and diced

⅓ cup slivered almonds

¼ cup plain whole-milk Greek yogurt

¼ cup mayonnaise

1 tablespoon rice vinegar

2 teaspoons prepared wasabi paste

Grated zest of 1 lime

Freshly ground white pepper

2 ripe medium avocados, cut into ½-inch cubes

Preheat the oven to 425°F.

Arrange the beets in a single layer on a large piece of foil set on top of a large baking sheet. Generously coat them with olive oil and sprinkle with salt. Wrap the foil around the beets, creating a pouch, and transfer the baking sheet to the oven. Roast the beets for about 90 minutes, until tender and easily pierced with a knife. Let cool to room temperature.

In a large bowl, toss together the lettuces, edamame, cucumber, and slivered almonds. Set aside.

In a small bowl, whisk together the yogurt, mayonnaise, vinegar, wasabi, lime juice, ¼ teaspoon salt, and ¼ teaspoon white pepper. Set aside.

When the roasted beets are cool enough to handle, peel and chop them into ½-inch pieces. (You might want to wear plastic gloves while you do this if using red beets to avoid staining your hands.)

Add the beets to the salad. Add the dressing and avocado cubes and gently toss to coat. Season with salt and white pepper and serve.

PASTRAMI REUBEN WITH BRUSSELS SPROUT SLAW

Katz's Deli in New York City is famous for their Reubens. It stands to reason—they're towering piles of the juiciest pastrami topped with melty Swiss cheese and creamy Russian dressing. Brady is such a big fan of this combo that I knew I had to start making a version at home, but with a twist (of course). I added a fresh, crunchy, tangy Brussels sprout slaw that I toss with an apple vinegar–buttermilk–mayo combo; but I left the rest pretty much the same. I mean, you can't mess with a good thing too much.

To make these sandwiches a cinch to throw together, I serve mine cold. But you could just as easily melt some butter in a pan and griddle the assembled sandwiches until the bread is just browned and the cheese is melted.

Serves 6

FOR THE BRUSSELS SPROUT SLAW:

½ cup apple cider vinegar

3 cups shaved Brussels sprouts (about 12 ounces)

¼ cup mayonnaise

2 tablespoons buttermilk

4 teaspoons fresh lemon juice (from 1 lemon)

1 tablespoon sugar

1 teaspoon Dijon mustard

½ teaspoon celery salt

¼ teaspoon kosher salt

Dash of freshly ground black pepper

FOR THE RUSSIAN DRESSING:

1 cup mayonnaise

¼ cup ketchup

3 tablespoons pickle relish

1 tablespoon prepared horseradish, drained

½ teaspoon paprika

Kosher salt and freshly ground black pepper

TO ASSEMBLE:

12 slices pumpernickel bread

1½ pounds sliced pastrami (from your favorite local deli)

6 slices Swiss cheese

Dill pickles, for serving

For the Brussels sprout slaw: Bring the vinegar to a simmer in a large skillet or saucepan over medium heat. Add the Brussels sprouts and cook, stirring occasionally, until just soft, about 5 minutes. Remove from the heat.

In a large bowl, combine the mayonnaise, buttermilk, lemon juice, sugar, mustard, celery salt, kosher salt, and pepper. Whisk until blended and smooth. Add the Brussels sprouts and toss to coat. Refrigerate overnight or for at least 4 hours.

For the Russian dressing: In a small bowl, combine the mayonnaise, ketchup, pickle relish, horseradish, and paprika. Season with salt and pepper. Refrigerate the dressing until ready to use.

To assemble: Spread some Russian dressing over a slice of bread. Add 3 slices of pastrami, enough slaw to cover the pastrami, and 1 slice of Swiss cheese. Spread some dressing over a second slice of bread and place it dressing-side down on top of the cheese. Cut in half. Repeat to make 5 more sandwiches.

Serve with dill pickles.

Pastrami Reuben with Brussels Sprout Slaw (p. 70)

RUSTIC TURKEY PANINI WITH BRIE, APPLES & WATERCRESS

Give me a slice of Brie and a slice of apple, and I'll be one happy lady. It's a classic pairing that hits that sweet-salty note I'm such a big fan of—plus, I love how the soft Brie melts against the crisp apple in your mouth. This sandwich takes that cheese-board vibe to the next level with peppery watercress, smoked turkey, and a gloss of rich walnut oil.

Serves 2

2 tablespoons walnut oil

2 teaspoons chopped fresh thyme

4 (½-inch-thick) slices whole wheat country bread

2 ounces Brie cheese, thinly sliced

4 ounces thinly sliced smoked turkey

1 Granny Smith apple or pear, cored and thinly sliced

1 small bunch fresh watercress, tough stems removed

½ teaspoon fresh lemon juice

Freshly ground black pepper

Preheat a panini press, griddle, or large skillet.

In a small bowl, mix together the walnut oil and thyme. Liberally brush one side of each slice of bread with the oil mixture. Turn 2 of the slices oiled-side down. Top each of these two slices with one-quarter of the Brie, half the turkey, half the apple slices, and a few sprigs of watercress. Drizzle with lemon juice and the remaining thyme oil. Sprinkle with a few cracks of pepper and put the remaining Brie on top.

Place the other 2 bread slices on top, oiled-sides up, and carefully transfer one sandwich to the panini press, griddle, or skillet. If you aren't using a panini press, place a heavy pan on top of the sandwich. Cook the sandwich until the bread is golden and toasted, the apple and turkey are heated through, and the cheese has melted, 3 to 4 minutes per side. Repeat with the second sandwich.

Cut each sandwich in half and serve immediately.

FRESH MOZZARELLA, PROSCIUTTO & FIG BAGUETTE

Baguette sandwiches are the Swiss Army knife of lunch—portable, handy, and great in infinite combinations. While you can't go wrong with any stack of your favorite ingredients on fresh, crusty bread, I love this pairing of mild mozzarella, salty prosciutto, and sweet fig jam. Parcel these up in parchment and twine, rustle up a bottle of rosé, and you have yourself a picnic!

Serves 4

1 French baguette,
halved lengthwise

¾ cup Fig Jam (page 11)
or store-bought jam

10 slices prosciutto

2 (8-ounce) balls fresh mozzarella,
sliced into ¼-inch-thick rounds

Spread the baguette halves generously with the jam. Arrange the prosciutto slices and mozzarella rounds on one half, and top with the other half. Cut the sandwich crosswise into 4 pieces.

LOBSTER BLT LETTUCE WRAPS

BLTs are probably one of Brady's favorite sandwiches—at least, they were until he had an acting job where he had to eat about fifty of them in an afternoon. When he finally started craving them again, I changed it up for him by taking another favorite—the lobster roll—and creating the mother lode of all sandwiches. But instead of making it an all-out indulgence, I swapped out the traditional buttered brioche for lettuce wraps. Believe me, you won't miss the bread when you have fresh lobster, bacon, and mayo.

Serves 6

6 bacon slices

4 fresh live Maine lobsters (about 1½ pounds each)

6 tablespoons (¾ stick) unsalted butter, melted

2 to 4 tablespoons fresh lemon juice (from about 3 lemons), plus more to taste

1 tablespoon chopped fresh tarragon, plus more for garnish

Kosher salt and freshly ground black pepper

6 large butter lettuce leaves, washed and dried

3 Roma (plum) tomatoes, halved lengthwise and thinly sliced

Preheat the oven to 375°F. Line a rimmed baking sheet with foil and set a wire rack on top.

Arrange the bacon on the rack in a single layer. Cook the bacon in the oven for 30 to 45 minutes, until crispy. Remove from the oven and let cool. When cool enough to handle, coarsely chop and set aside.

Insert a steamer basket into a large steamer pot. Fill the pot with 2 to 3 inches of water and bring to a boil over high heat. Meanwhile, fill a large bowl with ice water. Carefully add the lobsters to the steamer, piling them on top of one another. Cover and reduce the heat to medium. Cook for about 12 minutes, until the lobsters are bright red-orange. Immediately transfer the lobsters to the ice bath to stop them from cooking. Set aside to cool completely.

Once the lobsters are cool enough to handle, break off their tails, knuckles, and claws. (YouTube can be your friend here!) Use a lobster cracker to crack the shells and extract the meat. You should have about 1½ pounds of meat. Reserve the shells, legs, and carcasses for another use; I like to freeze mine to use for lobster bisque.

Keep the lobster meat in whole pieces or chop it up for a more traditional look. In a large bowl, toss the lobster with the chopped bacon, melted butter, 2 tablespoons of the lemon juice, and the tarragon. Season with salt, pepper, and more lemon juice to taste.

Top each lettuce leaf with 3 slices of tomato. Divide the lobster mixture among the lettuce wraps and sprinkle with tarragon before serving.

CRAB SALAD–STUFFED AVOCADOS

Salads don't need to begin and end with lettuce. For this version I drew inspiration from the ingredients of a crab cake—jumbo lump crab, mayo and sour cream, lemon juice, and Old Bay—and gave them a fresh, springy twist with crisp raw fennel, scallion, and chives. While this alone would be the perfect light lunch on a bed of greens, I love serving it over avocado halves. It's simple and satisfying enough for a quick bite, but could easily hold its own in an elegant spread for a ladies' lunch or baby/bridal shower.

Serves 6

2 pounds jumbo lump crabmeat, picked over to remove any shells or cartilage

½ medium fennel bulb, cored and finely chopped

3 scallions, finely chopped

¼ cup mayonnaise

2 tablespoons sour cream

2 tablespoons fresh lemon juice (from 1 lemon)

2 teaspoons Old Bay seasoning

2 tablespoons chopped fresh chives

Kosher salt and freshly ground black pepper

3 ripe medium avocados, pitted and peeled

Chive blossoms, for garnish

In a medium bowl, combine the crabmeat, fennel, and scallions. In a separate small bowl, whisk together the mayonnaise, sour cream, lemon juice, Old Bay, and 1 tablespoon of the chives until blended. Season with salt and pepper to taste. Pour over the crabmeat and gently toss to coat.

To serve, scoop a dollop of the crab salad into the hollow of each avocado half. Garnish with the remaining 1 tablespoon chives.

FRIED CHICKEN
WITH PICKLE & POTATO SALAD

There's nothing like perfectly crispy fried chicken straight out of the pan, still glistening with all that finger-lickin' goodness. But you know what else is crazy delicious? Packing it up for a picnic and having it at room temperature—especially paired with creamy, tangy Pickle & Potato Salad.

My secret for nailing the most tender, juicy fried chicken is soaking the meat in buttermilk and a little hot sauce first, which infuses the chicken with flavor and also acts like a kind of brine, helping to make the meat tender. Then it gets tossed with a cornmeal-panko combination, fried to golden perfection, and finished in the oven so the meat is guaranteed to be cooked through. If you're feeling a little naughty, you could whip up a batch using boneless drumettes and use them to garnish a round of Bloody Caesars (page 18).

Serves 6 to 8

4 cups buttermilk

2 tablespoons hot sauce (see Note, page 82)

1 (5-pound) chicken, portioned into 10 pieces (ask your butcher to help you, if necessary)

1 cup all-purpose flour

1 cup panko bread crumbs

1 tablespoon kosher salt, plus more for sprinkling

2 teaspoons freshly ground black pepper

Peanut oil, for frying

Pickle & Potato Salad (recipe follows)

In a large container with a lid, whisk together the buttermilk and hot sauce. Submerge the chicken in the mixture, cover, and refrigerate overnight. (This step is crucial for moist, delicious fried chicken!)

Line a rimmed baking sheet with foil and set a wire rack on top. Remove the chicken from the marinade and set it on the rack to drain any excess marinade. Set aside.

In a shallow dish, whisk together the flour, bread crumbs, salt, and pepper. One by one, dredge the chicken pieces in the flour mixture, tapping them to allow any excess batter to fall off the skin. Return the coated chicken to the rack.

Preheat the oven to 350°F. Line a large baking sheet with paper towels.

Pour 2 inches of peanut oil into a Dutch oven or large pot, making sure the oil does come more than halfway up the sides of the pot. Heat the oil over medium-high heat to 350°F.

Carefully slide the chicken into the oil a few pieces at a time. (It is important that you don't add too much chicken to the pot, or the oil temperature will drop and the chicken won't crisp up as well.) Use tongs or a spider to turn the chicken every 1 to 2 minutes, until it turns a deep golden brown. Cooking times vary depending on which part of the chicken you're working with: Wings should cook for about 10 minutes, while breasts, thighs, and legs should take about 12 minutes.

(Continued)

When done, a thermometer inserted into the thickest part of the chicken should reach 165°F. Transfer the chicken to the paper towel–lined baking sheet and season immediately with salt.

If serving warm, let the chicken cool slightly before serving with the Pickle & Potato Salad. If packing it up to go, let it cool completely first or the steam will make the chicken soggy.

Note: Lately I've been obsessed with a small-batch brand of hot sauce called The Kitchen Garden, which you can find on Etsy.

PICKLE & POTATO SALAD

I love pickles! I can't get enough of their salty, briny acidity, which is why I also include a little of their juice in this potato salad. It helps this salad feel lighter and brighter, while the eggs keep things creamy and rich.

Serves 6

1½ pounds tricolored small potatoes

1½ teaspoons kosher salt, plus more for the potatoes

½ cup mayonnaise

¼ cup chopped sweet pickles

3 tablespoons pickle juice (from the jar)

1 tablespoon yellow mustard

¼ teaspoon freshly ground black pepper, plus more to taste

5 hard-boiled eggs, peeled and chopped

½ medium red onion, thinly sliced

2 tablespoons chopped fresh parsley, for garnish

Paprika, for garnish

Place the potatoes in a large pot and add enough cold water to cover them by 1 inch and a generous pinch of salt. Bring the water to a boil over medium-high heat and cook until the potatoes are fork-tender, 20 to 25 minutes. Drain the potatoes and let them rest until they're cool enough to handle. Cut each one in half.

In a small bowl, mix together the mayonnaise, sweet pickles, pickle juice, mustard, salt, and pepper.

In a separate large bowl, combine the halved potatoes, eggs, and red onion and toss with the dressing. Taste, adjust the seasoning, and garnish with the parsley and paprika.

DINNER
(AT TIFFANI'S)

Dinner is my favorite meal when it comes to feeding other people. There's this sense of release—work's done; everyone can kick off their shoes, have a glass of wine or a cocktail, and let go of the day. When I was a kid, my family had dinner together every night. We'd reminisce about what we were up to at school, hear about our parents' days, and then talk about what was next, what was coming tomorrow. It was like dinner meets family meeting. I've tried to preserve that tradition in my own family—even if it's a quick hi and bye over plain pasta and carrot sticks. (Hey, a mom's gotta do what a mom's gotta do!) Fancy or not, there is nothing more satisfying than putting something nourishing on the table and then sending everyone to bed feeling satisfied and cared for. And now that my daughter is older, I get her involved in preparing dinner. I love doing things where Harper can be right next to me helping, like rolling out pizza dough or stirring (the aforementioned) pasta in the pot. I've even started teaching her how to use a knife. It's absolutely true what they say—the more kids help with cooking, the more they want to eat what they make.

When it's the holidays, a special occasion, or just an evening with a few friends, I get everyone in the kitchen. I have such fond memories of my mom and my aunt spending the day cooking together and the kitchen buzzing with all the activity and chatter and laughter. It was as much a part of the celebration as the meal itself. I always try to bring that spirit to my entertaining for any meal, but dinner especially. So often people think that having people over for dinner needs to be overly formal. I'm all for adding polished touches, but that shouldn't mean the night feels forced or stiff. Your guests can get all dressed up and get their hands a little dirty in the kitchen. The table can be tablescaped up the wazoo and your kid can help do the place cards. The more you think of dinner entertaining as just another night around the table, another opportunity to connect and enjoy one another's company, another chance to show your love through a delicious plate of food, the more special an evening it will be.

BEAN & HAM HOCK STEW

This was a standby dish in my house that my mom would usually make on Sundays, so we could eat it throughout the week. She'd always use navy beans, which would get nice and creamy. And the secret to giving the beans the most deliciously deep, meaty flavor? A few ham hocks—a staple ingredient in my mom's kitchen, like so many other working class families', because they were cheap. Far be it for me to change a good thing, so I've stayed true to the original recipe. The only slight difference is that I've added bay leaves and a touch of herbes de Provence, an aromatic blend of dried rosemary, thyme, oregano, and lavender.

Serves 4 to 6

1 pound dried navy beans, rinsed and picked over

⅛ teaspoon baking soda

1 tablespoon vegetable oil

4 meaty ham hocks (about 3 pounds)

1 medium yellow onion, finely chopped

1 medium fennel bulb, cored and finely chopped

4 garlic cloves, minced

¼ cup white wine

3 bay leaves

1 teaspoon herbes de Provence

½ teaspoon kosher salt

½ teaspoon freshly ground black pepper

2 tablespoons chopped fresh parsley, for garnish

In a large bowl or pot, combine the beans, baking soda, and 3 quarts water and set aside to soak overnight. Drain and rinse the beans.

In a large stockpot, heat the vegetable oil over medium-high heat. Add the ham hocks and sear until browned, 4 to 5 minutes per side. Remove from the pan and set aside.

Reduce the heat to medium and add the onion and fennel. Cook, stirring, until softened, about 5 minutes. Add the garlic and cook until fragrant, about 1 minute. Pour in the wine. Using a wooden spoon, scrape up whatever ham hock and onion bits may have stuck to the bottom of the pot. Simmer until the liquid has cooked off, about 2 minutes.

Add the bay leaves, herbes de Provence, salt, pepper, and 2 quarts water. Return the ham hocks to the pot and bring the water to a full boil. Reduce the heat to low, cover, and simmer until the ham hocks are tender, about 2 hours.

Stir in the beans and cook, covered, until the meat is falling off the bones, about 1 hour more. Transfer the ham hocks to a plate to cool; continue cooking the beans. Discard the skin and bones from the ham hocks and shred the meat. Return the meat to the pot and cook until the beans are tender and the stew has thickened, another 45 to 60 minutes.

Garnish each serving with fresh parsley.

THAI-STYLE
SHRIMP & COCONUT SOUP

I'd eaten versions of this dish whenever we went out for Thai food in California, but when I finally had it in Thailand, *that* was the real "aha" moment. I couldn't believe how aromatic the broth was—loaded with lemongrass, cilantro, Thai lime leaves (sometimes referred to as kaffir lime leaves), and galangal, a slightly sweeter version of ginger (though ginger is a perfect substitute). It's rich and luscious thanks to coconut milk, but not at all heavy. And the whole thing was spiked with savory fish sauce and spicy Thai chili paste. Once I got home, I immediately got to work re-creating it because I knew I'd always need a way to satisfy that craving. You may need to track down some of these ingredients (lemongrass, lime leaves, galangal) at an Asian market or specialty spice shop, or even online, but I promise it's worth it!

Serves 4

1½ quarts chicken broth

½ stalk lemongrass, tender bottom portion smashed with the back of a knife and sliced into ¼-inch pieces

1 (1½-inch) piece fresh galangal or ginger, peeled and thinly sliced crosswise

8 fresh Thai lime leaves, torn and lightly bruised

6 ounces unsweetened full-fat coconut milk

6 ounces button mushrooms (about 2 cups), quartered

1 small red bell pepper, diced

3 tablespoons red Thai chili paste (I like nam prik pao)

2 tablespoons fish sauce

1 or 2 dried Thai chiles or 1 fresh Anaheim chile, seeded and thinly sliced

1 pound shrimp, peeled and deveined

4 teaspoons fresh lime juice (from about 1 lime)

1 teaspoon palm or light brown sugar

¼ cup lightly packed fresh cilantro leaves

Chili oil

In a stockpot, bring the chicken broth to a gentle boil over medium heat. Add the lemongrass, galangal, and lime leaves and reduce the heat to low so the liquid is barely simmering. Cook until the broth is well infused with aromatic flavor, 20 to 25 minutes. Add the coconut milk, mushrooms, bell pepper, chili paste, fish sauce, and dried chiles and simmer, stirring, until the vegetables are tender, about another 5 minutes. Add the shrimp. Cook, stirring occasionally, until the shrimp are bright pink and cooked through, about 1 minute. Remove from the heat.

Season the soup to your liking with the lime juice, sugar, and fish sauce. Stir in the cilantro leaves.

Serve with the chili oil if you want to make the soup spicier—be sure to add it a few drops at a time!

90

FOUR-BEAN CHILI
WITH SKILLET CORN BREAD
& ALL THE FIXINS

Harper is, shall we say, a *selective* eater. We don't always see eye to eye on what constitutes a proper meal. But what I've found is that the more control she has over what she eats, the more she's interested in trying something new. Putting out a big pot of chili and a ton of different topping options that she can mix and match to her heart's content is a total slam-dunk—and everyone else is a big fan too. It's fantastic for a weeknight dinner because you can repurpose the leftovers all kinds of ways, like scooped over burgers or hot dogs, or heaped on top of Bacon Fat Fries (page 190). (Somewhere my husband's ears just perked up!) It's also the perfect make-ahead dish for a crowd. And while it's vegetarian, no one will miss the meat because it's loaded with hearty beans and gets tons of deep, smoky flavor from spices like chili powder, chipotle, cumin, coriander, and cayenne. (Though you can always add bacon, ground beef, or ground turkey, which I sometimes do for myself.) As for toppings, I love offering the classics: corn and/or tortilla chips; sour cream or plain Greek yogurt; chopped chives, onions, and scallions; jalapeños; bell peppers; shredded cheese; and crispy bacon. Set everything out with a batch of Skillet Corn Bread—for sopping up every last morsel from the bowl—and everyone will be feeling at home in no time.

Serves 4 to 6

¼ cup extra-virgin olive oil

2 large yellow onions,
finely chopped

Kosher salt and freshly ground
black pepper

1 (6-ounce) can tomato paste

¼ cup chili powder

4 garlic cloves, minced

1 teaspoon chipotle powder

1 teaspoon ground cumin

1 teaspoon ground coriander

½ teaspoon cayenne pepper

6 cups vegetable broth

1 (28-ounce) can diced tomatoes,
with their juices

2 cups frozen corn

1 (15-ounce) can red kidney beans,
drained and rinsed

1 (15-ounce) can black beans,
drained and rinsed

1 (15-ounce) can pinto beans,
drained and rinsed

1 (15-ounce) can chickpeas, drained
and rinsed

2 teaspoons Worcestershire sauce

Skillet Corn Bread
(recipe follows)

(Continued)

TOPPINGS BAR:

**Sour cream or plain whole-milk
Greek yogurt**

Shredded cheddar cheese

Chopped cooked bacon

Chopped yellow onion

Chopped fresh chives

Seeded and minced jalapeños

Corn chips, such as Fritos

**Homemade Tortilla Chips
(page 201)**

In a Dutch oven or large pot, heat 2 tablespoons of the olive oil over medium heat. Add the onions and a pinch each of salt and pepper and cook, stirring, until soft, about 3 minutes. Stir in the remaining 2 tablespoons olive oil, the tomato paste, chili powder, garlic, chipotle, cumin, coriander, and cayenne. Cook, stirring, until the spices and tomato paste toast, 1 to 2 minutes. Add the broth, diced tomatoes and their juices, corn, kidney beans, black beans, pinto beans, chickpeas, Worcestershire, and 1 tablespoon salt. Bring to a simmer and cook until the chili thickens, about 1 hour. Taste and adjust the seasonings.

Spoon into bowls, heap with your desired toppings, and serve with Skillet Corn Bread.

SKILLET CORN BREAD

The secret to great corn bread is browning your butter in the skillet first and then pouring the batter into the buttered skillet without wiping it out, giving the bread a richer, nuttier flavor. I also like using maple syrup to sweeten as opposed to all sugar, so it's not too sweet.

Serves 4 to 6

**¾ cup (1½ sticks) unsalted butter,
plus more for serving**

1 cup buttermilk

⅓ cup maple syrup

¼ cup whole milk

3 large eggs

1½ cups fine yellow cornmeal

½ cup whole wheat flour

½ cup all-purpose flour

¼ cup sugar

1½ tablespoons baking powder

1½ teaspoons kosher salt

½ teaspoon baking soda

Preheat the oven to 375°F.

Melt the butter in a 10-inch cast-iron skillet over medium heat. Swirl the pan to coat the sides and bottom. Cook, making sure not to burn the butter, until the foam disappears and the butter is a light brown color, 2 to 3 minutes. You'll know the butter is ready when it starts giving off a nutty aroma. Pour the brown butter into a large bowl and set the skillet aside without wiping it out.

In a separate large bowl, whisk together the buttermilk, maple syrup, and whole milk. Whisk in the eggs. Add the cornmeal, flours, sugar, baking powder, salt, and baking soda and whisk until combined.

Pour the batter into the skillet. Bake for 20 minutes, or until the sides are golden brown and a toothpick inserted into the center comes out clean. Allow to cool and serve warm with butter.

BEET RISOTTO

Risotto is just one of those dishes that seems so fancy and complicated but is actually beyond easy to make. It's just Arborio rice—which naturally gets creamy when cooked—plus stock, butter, cheese, and a little love and attention with a spoon. That's it! But what I especially like about risotto is that it's the perfect canvas for adding in just about any vegetable—roasted squash, sautéed wild mushrooms, sweet corn . . . For this version, I went with roasted beets, which gives the risotto a gorgeous, gem-toned color.

Serves 2 or 3

1½ pounds red beets, washed and dried

4 tablespoons extra-virgin olive oil

Kosher salt and freshly ground black pepper

6 cups chicken broth

3 tablespoons unsalted butter

2 shallots, finely chopped

3 garlic cloves, minced

1½ cups Arborio rice

¼ cup dry white wine

¼ cup freshly grated Parmesan cheese

Preheat the oven to 425°F.

Set the beets on a large sheet of foil set on top of a baking sheet. Toss the beets with 2 tablespoons of the olive oil and a generous pinch each of salt and pepper. Wrap the foil around the beets to form a pouch and transfer the baking sheet to the oven. Roast for 40 to 55 minutes, depending on the size of the beets, until they are tender when pierced with a paring knife. Set aside to cool.

In a small saucepan, bring the broth to a boil over medium heat. Reduce the heat to medium-low and simmer. (You're just keeping the broth warm while you prepare the risotto.)

In a large high-sided skillet or saucepot, melt the butter in the remaining 2 tablespoons olive oil over medium heat. Add the shallots and cook, stirring, until soft, 3 to 4 minutes. Add the garlic and cook, stirring, until fragrant, another 30 seconds. Stir in the rice and cook until it is lightly toasted and starts to turn opaque, 2 to 3 minutes. Pour in the wine and cook until it's almost completely evaporated, about 4 minutes. Reduce the heat to medium-low. Add a ladleful of the warm stock and stir continuously until the stock has been almost completely absorbed. Repeat this step until the rice is al dente—tender but still firm to the bite—and creamy, about 40 minutes. You may not use all the stock. Remove the risotto from the heat and stir in the Parmesan.

When the roasted beets are cool enough to handle, peel and chop them into ¼-inch pieces. (You might want to wear plastic gloves while you do this if using red beets to avoid staining your hands.)

Reserving ½ cup for garnish, stir the cubed beets into the risotto. Season with salt and pepper and garnish with the reserved beets. Serve immediately.

KITCHEN SINK FRIED RICE

This is the ultimate dish for any parent whose kid is a die-hard fan of plain rice—and maybe, just maybe, doesn't like eating their veggies. What I found is that by chopping vegetables really fine so they mimic the size and texture of the rice, then frying it all up so it's ten kinds of crispy goodness, my kids are game for eating every last bite. The beauty of this dish is that you can use just about any veg that's lying around in your crisper—carrots, broccoli, snap peas, squash, bell pepper, zucchini—then top it with crepe-like strips of cooked egg and be done. Or if you want to dress it up a little bit more, you can add some Asian ingredients like garlic, ginger, and soy sauce, which give everything a salty, savory depth of flavor.

Serves 4

3 tablespoons unsalted butter

2 large eggs, beaten

1 garlic clove, minced

1 teaspoon fresh ginger, minced

¼ cup finely diced yellow onion

¼ cup finely diced carrot

¼ cup finely diced zucchini

¼ cup finely diced red bell pepper

3 cups cooked brown rice

2 tablespoons Shaoxing wine, rice wine, or sherry

2 tablespoons soy sauce

¼ cup fresh or frozen peas

2 small scallions, finely chopped

2 teaspoons untoasted sesame oil

1 teaspoon white sesame seeds, toasted (see Note, page 38)

In a small nonstick pan, melt 1 tablespoon of the butter over medium heat. Swirl the pan to coat the sides and bottom. Pour the beaten eggs into the pan to form a thin, crepe-like layer. Cook until almost cooked through, 3 to 4 minutes. Flip the egg over to cook the other side for a minute. Transfer the egg to a cutting board and let it cool slightly, then cut it into thin strips. Set aside.

Melt 1 tablespoon of the remaining butter in a large skillet or wok over medium-high heat. Add the garlic and ginger and cook, stirring, until fragrant, about 30 seconds. Add the onion, carrot, zucchini, and bell pepper and cook, stirring continuously, until the vegetables are slightly softened, 2 to 3 minutes. Push the vegetables to one side of the pan and add the remaining 1 tablespoon butter. Add the rice and cook, stirring, for 2 to 3 minutes, then combine the rice with the vegetables. Deglaze the pan with the Shaoxing wine and stir, scraping up anything stuck to the bottom of the pan. Reduce the heat to medium and cook until the wine has evaporated, about 2 minutes.

Add the soy sauce and stir in the peas. Cook, stirring continuously to keep the mixture moving, until all the liquid has evaporated, 3 to 5 minutes. Add the egg strips and half the scallions. Stir to heat the eggs and scallions through. Remove from the heat and stir in the sesame oil. Transfer to a serving dish and garnish with the remaining scallions and the toasted sesame seeds.

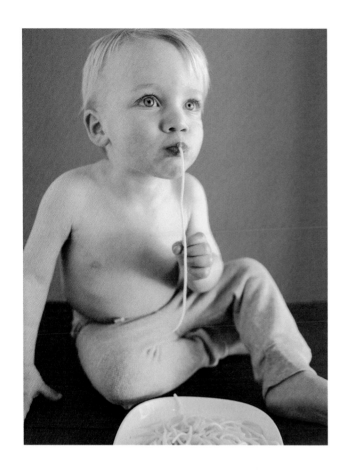
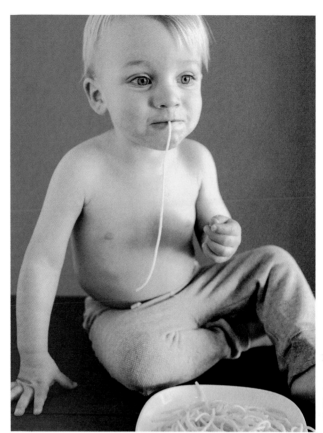
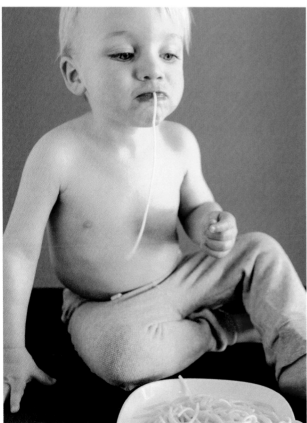
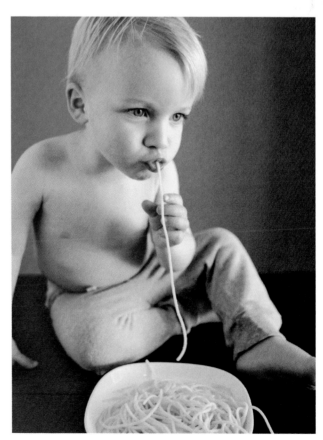

SPRING PEA & PANCETTA CARBONARA

The kids love this dish because it's essentially like mac 'n' cheese with bits of salty pancetta, and I love it because I get to sneak in lots of fresh peas. And it's great for dressing up, too. Make it in a pretty oven-to-table dish for a big hit at dinner parties.

Serves 4

1 pound spaghetti

1½ cups fresh or frozen peas

1 large egg

½ cup heavy cream

Kosher salt and freshly ground black pepper

6 ounces pancetta, chopped

2 tablespoons extra-virgin olive oil

1 shallot, finely diced

4 garlic cloves, minced

Freshly grated Parmesan cheese, for garnish

Coarsely chopped fresh mint, for garnish

Bring a large pot of salted water to a boil. Cook the pasta according to the package instructions and add the peas during the last minute of cooking. Drain in a colander and set aside.

In a small bowl, whisk together the egg and cream. Season with a pinch each of salt and pepper.

In a large saucepan, gently cook the pancetta over medium-low heat until it browns and the fat renders, 10 to 15 minutes. Using a slotted spoon, transfer the pancetta to a paper towel–lined plate or tray, leaving the rendered fat in the pan.

Add the olive oil to the pan with the rendered fat and heat over medium heat. Add the shallot and ½ teaspoon salt. Cook, stirring, until the shallot is soft and golden, about 5 minutes. Add the garlic and cook, stirring, until just fragrant, about 1 minute. Return the pancetta to the pan, then add the pasta and peas. Slowly stream in the egg and cream sauce and toss lightly to evenly coat the pasta. Remove from the heat, transfer to a serving dish, and garnish with the Parmesan and fresh mint.

HOLT'S FAVORITE BAKED MAC 'N' CHEESE

One of the first times I was visiting one of my best friends down in South Carolina, we went to a barbecue spot and were served an enormous slice of macaroni and cheese. Up until then, I'd only seen the kind that got mixed up in a pot, so the idea of a casserole-style version that was super gooey in the middle, slightly crispy along the edges, and topped with bubbling, browned cheese seemed almost too good to be true. So now I make a version with traditional cheddar, plus ricotta to keep things super creamy, a pinch of mustard powder to get that classic mac 'n' cheese yellow, and butternut squash for a little sweetness and even creamier body—and some vitamins, too, but no need to tell anyone that.

Serves 4 to 6

4 tablespoons (½ stick) unsalted butter, plus more for greasing

1¼ cups cubed peeled butternut squash

½ pound cavatappi pasta

3 tablespoons all-purpose flour

2 cups whole milk

2¼ teaspoons mustard powder

1 teaspoon kosher salt, plus more for the pasta water

¼ teaspoon freshly ground white pepper

3½ cups coarsely grated mild cheddar cheese (about 10 ounces)

½ cup Homemade Ricotta (page 276) or store-bought

Preheat the oven to 400°F. Grease a 2-quart baking dish with butter.

Insert a steamer basket into a large steamer pot. Add 2 inches of water and bring to a boil. Put the squash in the steamer, cover, and cook until very, very soft, about 15 minutes. Transfer to a food processor and process until smooth. Set aside ½ cup of the squash; freeze the rest for another use.

Bring a large pot of salted water to a boil over high heat. Add the cavatappi and cook until firm to the bite, about 8 minutes. Drain and set aside.

Melt the butter in a large, wide pot over medium-low heat. Sprinkle the flour over the butter and whisk, making a roux. Cook, whisking continuously, until the roux is light golden, about 5 minutes. Pour in the milk, whisking continuously. Increase the heat to medium-high and bring to a low boil, about 4 minutes. Reduce the heat to low and simmer until the sauce thickens and coats the back of a spoon, about 3 minutes. Add the mustard powder, salt, and pepper and stir. Add 3 cups of the cheddar in three or four batches, whisking to make sure the cheese is fully melted before adding the next. Stir in the ricotta and reserved ½ cup pureed squash. When the mixture is fully blended, remove from the heat.

Add the cavatappi to the sauce and stir to coat. Transfer the mixture to the baking dish and scatter ½ cup cheddar evenly over the top. Place on a rimmed baking sheet and bake for 25 to 30 minutes, until the cheese is browned and bubbly. Let cool for 15 minutes before serving.

COWBOY POUTINE

Traditional poutine, as you'd have it in Montreal, is French fries slathered with gravy and dotted with cheese curds. It's pretty hard to improve on this dish, but one time when I was there with Brady, one of our favorite restaurants offered a version with pulled duck on top. Needless to say, it was insanely delicious. It gave me the idea to offer my own down-home spin, drawing inspiration from Brady's Texas roots. I've kept the cheese curds but swapped the gravy for baked beans and the duck for BBQ pulled pork. And it all gets heaped on Bacon Fat Fries (page 190). You heard me right. If you make these, please save me a plate.

Serves 4 to 6

FOR THE BBQ PULLED PORK:

2 tablespoons smoked paprika

1 tablespoon onion powder

1 tablespoon garlic powder

1 tablespoon ground cumin

1 teaspoon cayenne pepper

Kosher salt and freshly ground black pepper

1 (3-pound) bone-in pork shoulder (Boston butt)

2 medium yellow onions, cut into thick slices

1 cup barbecue sauce

¼ cup chicken broth

Light brown sugar

Apple cider vinegar

FOR THE BBQ BAKED BEANS:

5 or 6 bacon slices (8 ounces)

½ medium yellow onion, coarsely chopped

3 garlic cloves, minced

2 (15-ounce) cans baked beans, drained and rinsed

2 tablespoons molasses

¼ cup light brown sugar

TO ASSEMBLE:

2 cups Bacon Fat Fries (page 190)

½ cup cheddar cheese curds (see Note, page 109), broken into bite-size pieces

(Continued)

For the BBQ pulled pork: In a small bowl, whisk together the smoked paprika, onion powder, garlic powder, cumin, cayenne, and 1 teaspoon salt. Massage the mixture into the skin of the pork and wrap the pork tightly in plastic wrap. Refrigerate overnight.

Scatter the onions over the bottom of a slow cooker. Unwrap the seasoned pork and place it on top of the onions, fat-side up. Pour the barbecue sauce and broth over the pork. Cover and cook on Low for 9 to 11 hours or on High for 5 to 7 hours. You'll know the shoulder is done when it is fork-tender and the meat falls off the bone. Leaving the onions and liquid in the slow cooker, gently transfer the cooked pork to a large baking dish and cover loosely with foil. Let cool.

For the sauce: Using a large spoon or gravy separator, skim the fat off the top of the liquid left in the slow cooker. Using an immersion blender, puree the onions and liquid directly in the food processor until you have a smooth, thick sauce. Season with salt and pepper and, if desired, a pinch of brown sugar or a splash of vinegar. Set the sauce aside.

When the pork is cool enough to handle, use two forks to shred it into long pieces about the size of French fries. Discard any bones, visible fat, or gristle. Season with salt. Set aside 1 cup and refrigerate the rest for pulled pork sandwiches, enchiladas, or tacos. (It will keep for 3 to 4 days.)

For the BBQ baked beans: Preheat the oven to 350°F.

In a medium skillet, cook the bacon over medium heat until the fat renders and the bacon is golden brown on both sides but not yet crisp, about 4 minutes per side. Transfer to a paper towel–lined plate, leaving the fat in the pan. Let the bacon cool and then chop into ¼-inch pieces.

Add the onion to the pan with the bacon drippings and cook over medium heat, stirring, until tender and translucent, about 7 minutes. Add the garlic and cook, stirring, until fragrant, 1 to 2 minutes. Remove from the heat.

In a large bowl, combine the bacon, onion-garlic mixture, baked beans, molasses, brown sugar, and 1½ cups of the reserved sauce from the pulled pork. Pour the mixture into a 2-quart baking dish. Bake, uncovered, for about 1 hour, until the sauce has thickened and the beans are a rich dark brown color. Let cool for at least 10 minutes. Set aside 1 cup for serving and reserve the rest for later use, maybe tossed into your next salad, poured over grilled meat, or eaten as is. (The beans will keep in an airtight container in the fridge for 3 to 4 days.)

To assemble: Pile the Bacon Fat Fries on your serving dish. Top with 1 cup of the pulled pork, 1 cup of the baked beans, and ½ cup of the cheese curds. Pour ½ cup of the reserved sauce from the pulled pork over the entire dish, grab your cowboy boots, and serve immediately.

Note: It may not be possible to find cheese curds at your local market. If that's the case for you, don't give up on this dish! Just substitute the same amount of cubed cheddar cheese.

NOT-YOUR-MAMA'S TURKEY MEAT LOAF AND SOUR CREAM MASHED POTATOES

Not to knock my mom's meat loaf—a fixture on our weeknight dinner table—but I wanted to take this usually heavy meal to a lighter place. I use turkey instead of beef and/or pork and add oats instead of bread crumbs as a binder. Plus, it gets a kick of hot sauce, so while this meat loaf might be healthier, it definitely doesn't skimp on flavor.

Serves 4

2 tablespoons extra-virgin olive oil

1 medium yellow onion, chopped

2 pounds ground turkey

1½ cups old-fashioned oats

2 large eggs

¼ cup Worcestershire sauce

½ cup ketchup, plus more for topping

1½ teaspoons tomato paste

Hot sauce

2 teaspoons kosher salt

Freshly ground black pepper

Sour Cream Mashed Potatoes (recipe follows), for serving

Preheat the oven to 350°F.

In a small skillet, heat the olive oil over medium heat. Add the onion and cook, stirring, until tender and fragrant, about 6 minutes. Let cool.

In a large bowl, combine the ground turkey, oats, eggs, Worcestershire, ketchup, and tomato paste. Season with a dash or two of the hot sauce (depending on how hot you like things), the salt, and a few cracks of pepper (again, to your liking). Add the cooled onion and combine the ingredients with your (clean) hands.

Transfer the meat loaf mixture to an 8-by-4-inch loaf pan. Press it down until the meat is flat and level. Top with as much ketchup as you like.

Bake for 45 to 50 minutes, until a meat thermometer registers 165°F. Let cool for 5 minutes.

Slice and serve with Sour Cream Mashed Potatoes.

(Continued)

SOUR CREAM MASHED POTATOES

This is a family heirloom of a recipe. We always had it on the table at the holidays, and I couldn't wait to fix myself a heaping bowl. In fact, I like them so much that any other mashed potatoes just don't do it for me. These get nice and creamy from sour cream, cream cheese, and butter, of course. And then they're whipped, so the texture is anything but heavy. I also considered calling these "24-hour potatoes" because they're the perfect do-ahead dish. You can cook the potatoes, mash 'em, and whip 'em the day before, then pop them in the oven right before serving, so they come to the table bubbling and golden.

Serves 4 to 6

4 tablespoons (½ stick) unsalted butter, sliced, plus more for greasing

8 to 10 russet potatoes, peeled and quartered

Kosher salt

1 (8-ounce) package cream cheese, at room temperature

1 cup sour cream

2 tablespoons chopped fresh chives

Freshly ground black pepper

Grease a 3-quart baking dish with butter.

Place the potatoes in a large pot and add just enough cold water to cover. Add a generous pinch of salt. Bring the water to a boil and cook the potatoes until they're soft and fork-tender, 10 to 15 minutes. Drain.

In the bowl of a stand mixer fitted with the paddle attachment, combine the potatoes, cream cheese, and sour cream and start to beat on low speed, increasing to medium as ingredients combine, until smooth. Stir in the chives by hand and season with salt and pepper. Transfer the mixture to the prepared baking dish and top evenly with the butter slices. Cover with foil and refrigerate until ready to bake.

Preheat the oven to 325°F. Remove the baking dish from the fridge 30 minutes before baking to take the chill off the potatoes.

Bake, still covered with foil, for 15 minutes. Uncover and bake for another 20 minutes, or until the potatoes are heated through. Serve hot!

ROASTED CHICKEN POTPIE

This recipe is just dreamy—the perfect antidote to a dreary, cold day when you just want something warm and savory and filling. It's called comfort food for a reason! Using roasted chicken gives the potpie an extra layer of flavor, as do the sweet root vegetables in the filling (carrots and parsnips are my favorite root veg combo, but you could use any other varieties), and a bit of salty Parmesan in the crust. You could make one large potpie in a baking dish, if you're putting this out for a family-style meal, or you could make individual servings if you want a more polished presentation for company. I particularly love serving them that way at a dinner where everyone's expecting something fussy and fancy. Believe me, no one's ever disappointed!

Serves 6

FOR THE CRUST:

2½ cups all-purpose flour

1 cup (2 sticks) unsalted butter, cut to ½-inch cubes

¼ cup finely grated Parmesan cheese

Pinch of kosher salt

FOR THE ROAST CHICKEN:

3 pounds bone-in, skin-on chicken thighs, patted dry

2 tablespoons extra-virgin olive oil

½ teaspoon paprika

1 teaspoon kosher salt

½ teaspoon freshly ground black pepper

½ teaspoon granulated garlic

FOR THE FILLING:

6 tablespoons (¾ stick) unsalted butter

1 large onion, finely chopped

Kosher salt and freshly ground black pepper

3 medium carrots, sliced into ¼-inch-thick coins

1 small fennel bulb, quartered, cored, and sliced crosswise into ¼-inch-thick pieces

1 parsnip, peeled and sliced into ¼-inch-thick coins

4 garlic cloves, minced

6 tablespoons all-purpose flour

¼ cup dry sherry

4 cups chicken broth, plus more as needed

¼ cup whole milk

¾ cup frozen peas

3 tablespoons finely chopped fresh flat-leaf parsley leaves

2 teaspoons chopped fresh thyme

1 large egg

(Continued)

For the crust: In a food processor, combine the flour, butter, Parmesan, and salt. Pulse until the mixture resembles fine gravel. Add ¼ to ½ cup water, a few tablespoons at a time, until the dough comes together and forms a ball. Turn out the dough onto a lightly floured surface and shape it into a disk. Wrap it in plastic wrap and refrigerate for at least 30 minutes or until ready to use.

For the roast chicken: Preheat the oven to 325°F. Set a roasting rack inside a roasting pan.

In a large bowl, slather the chicken with the olive oil, paprika, salt, pepper, and granulated garlic. Set the chicken on the roasting rack. Roast until the skin is golden and crispy and a thermometer inserted into the thickest part of the thigh reaches 165°F, 45 to 60 minutes. Set aside to cool. When cool enough to handle, remove the skin from the thighs. Pull the meat from the bones and tear it into bite-size pieces (discard the bones or use them for stock). Set aside 4 cups of meat and reserve the rest for later use (chicken salad, BBQ chicken sandwiches, chicken noodle soup).

For the filling: In a Dutch oven or large pot, melt the butter over medium-high heat. Add the onion, ½ teaspoon salt, and a dash of pepper and cook, stirring, until soft, about 3 minutes. Add the carrots, fennel, and parsnip and cook, stirring, until the vegetables are brightly colored, 2 to 3 minutes. Stir in the garlic and, when fragrant, stir in the flour. Cook, stirring continuously, for about 5 minutes.

Pour in the sherry and scrape up any bits stuck to the bottom of the pan. When the liquid has almost evaporated, stir in the broth and milk. Cook until thickened, about 10 minutes, or until the sauce coats the back of a spoon. If the sauce is too thick, add a splash of broth. Remove from the heat, stir in the reserved 4 cups shredded chicken, the peas, parsley, and thyme. Season with 1 tablespoon salt and ½ teaspoon pepper, or to taste.

To assemble: Preheat the oven to 350°F. Grease six ramekins or a 9-by-13-inch baking dish with olive oil.

On a lightly floured surface, roll the dough into a ¼-inch-thick rectangle, about 15 inches long and 11 inches wide. If using individual ramekins, cut 6 circles that are 1 inch larger in circumference than the ramekins. If using a single baking dish, cut the dough to that shape, leaving an extra inch around all sides.

Pour the filling into the ramekins or baking dish.

Lay the dough over the filling and trim it to ½ inch from the edge of the dish. Fold the overhang under itself to create a lip around the edge of the dish and use your fingers to flute the edges. Cut a 1-inch vent hole into a small pie or four to six 1-inch vent holes into a large pie.

In a small bowl, lightly beat the egg with 1 tablespoon water. Lightly brush the piecrust(s) with the egg wash.

Bake until the crust is golden brown and the filling is bubbling, about 60 minutes for large pies, 45 to 50 minutes for small pies. Serve immediately.

CITRUS BRICK CHICKEN WITH SWEET BARBECUE SAUCE

This recipe combines two of my favorite things about California: citrus and grilling just about anything, anytime. I especially love how cooking chicken over fire transforms the humble bird into its juiciest, most tender self. One trick is first letting the chicken soak in a citrus-based marinade so the meat picks up all kinds of flavor and also gets nice and tender. The other secret is grilling it whole. In order to get the chicken to lay flat on the grill and cook evenly, you'll need to take out its backbone, or "butterfly" it (don't worry, your butcher can do this for you!), then weight the chicken so it stays flat (hence the brick). Then my favorite finishing touch is serving the meat with a spicy-sweet barbecue sauce. Luckily, you can get great citrus just about anywhere year-round (especially in winter, when you're really craving that hit of sunny vitamin C), and no one says you can't wear a snowsuit while you grill!

Serves 4

FOR THE CITRUS MARINADE:

Grated zest and juice of
1 large navel orange

2 tablespoons honey

2 tablespoons chopped
fresh oregano

2 tablespoons sherry vinegar

Kosher salt and freshly ground
black pepper

½ cup canola oil

TO ASSEMBLE:

1 (4-pound) whole chicken,
butterflied (ask your butcher)

Sweet Barbecue Sauce
(recipe follows)

For the citrus marinade: In a medium bowl, whisk together the orange zest, orange juice, honey, oregano, vinegar, 2 large pinches of salt, and a pinch of pepper. Slowly stream in the canola oil while whisking so the mixture emulsifies.

To assemble: Place the chicken in a baking dish and pour in the marinade, turning the chicken to coat completely. Turn the chicken breast-side down in the marinade, cover with plastic wrap, and refrigerate overnight, or for at least 4 hours.

Remove the chicken from the dish, draining off any excess marinade, and place on a baking sheet. Pour about ¾ cup of the Sweet Barbecue Sauce into a small bowl and slather the sauce over both sides of the chicken. Set aside.

Heat a grill to medium-high. Cover two bricks with foil.

Place the chicken, skin-side up, on the grill and place the foil-covered bricks on top. Cook for 15 to 20 minutes. Remove the bricks to turn the chicken over, skin-side down. Set the bricks on top of the chicken and grill until the internal temperature reaches 165°F, about 10 minutes. Remove from the grill and let rest for about 10 minutes.

Cut into quarters and serve with the remaining Sweet Barbecue Sauce alongside.

(Continued)

SWEET BARBECUE SAUCE

Peaches and molasses add sweet notes to this otherwise tangy barbecue staple, and there's a hit of adobo sauce for smoky spice.

Makes 1½ cups

2 yellow peaches, peeled, pitted, and coarsely chopped

¾ cup peach nectar

½ cup ketchup

1 tablespoon molasses

1 tablespoon distilled white vinegar

2 teaspoons Dijon mustard

1 teaspoon Worcestershire sauce

½ teaspoon adobo sauce from a can of chipotle chiles

¼ teaspoon liquid smoke

In a large saucepan, combine the peaches, peach nectar, ketchup, molasses, vinegar, mustard, Worcestershire, adobo sauce, and liquid smoke. Bring to a boil over medium heat. Reduce the heat to low and simmer until the sauce has thickened and the flavors have melded, 25 to 30 minutes. Puree directly in the pot with an immersion blender, or transfer to a blender, let cool briefly, and blend until smooth (be careful when blending hot liquids). Let cool. Store in a lidded container in the fridge for up to 2 weeks.

Braised Tri Tip with Honey-Roasted
Carrots & Parsnips (page 126)

BRAISED TRI TIP WITH HONEY-ROASTED CARROTS & PARSNIPS

As my mother would say, this is a meal that sticks to your ribs. Tri tip is a cheaper, tougher cut, but it magically transforms as it braises low and slow in a broth that gets flavored with my secret ingredient: French onion soup mix. (Yep, you heard me right!) The deep, meaty flavor of the beef complements the sweetly caramelized root vegetables.

Serves 6 to 8

1 tablespoon vegetable oil

1 whole tri tip roast (about 3 pounds)

Kosher salt and freshly ground black pepper

2 yellow onions, thinly sliced

1 (1-ounce) packet French onion soup mix

2 sprigs fresh thyme

2 bay leaves

Honey-Roasted Carrots & Parsnips (recipe follows)

Preheat the oven to 325°F.

In a large pot or Dutch oven, heat the vegetable oil over medium-high heat. Season the roast with salt and pepper. Place the roast in the pot, fat-side down. Cook until browned, 3 minutes per side. Transfer to a plate. Drain off all but 2 tablespoons of the fat from the pot. Add the onions and cook, stirring occasionally, until they soften and start to brown, about 8 minutes. Stir in the soup mix, thyme, bay leaves, and 2 cups water. Return the meat to the pot with any juices that have collected on the plate and bring to a simmer.

Cover the pot with a lid and place it in the oven. Bake for 2½ to 3 hours, until the meat is fork-tender but not falling apart. Let the meat rest for 15 minutes. Skim off any excess fat from the braising liquid and discard the thyme sprigs and bay leaves.

Cut the tri tip into 1-inch-thick slices. Spoon the hot braising liquid over the slices and serve with Honey-Roasted Carrots & Parsnips.

HONEY-ROASTED
CARROTS & PARSNIPS

Carrots and parsnips are naturally sweet, which comes out even more when they're roasted—and shellacked with caramelized honey, plus a little soy sauce to balance it out. It's a beautiful, simple side that goes with just about any meal.

Serves 6 to 8

2 tablespoons extra-virgin olive oil

2 tablespoons honey

1 bunch medium carrots

1 bunch medium parsnips, peeled

Kosher salt and freshly ground black pepper

1 tablespoon soy sauce

1 tablespoon chopped fresh parsley

2 teaspoons black sesame seeds

Preheat the oven to 450°F. Line a large baking sheet with foil and heat it in the oven for 15 minutes.

In a large bowl, combine the olive oil and 1 tablespoon of the honey and toss with the carrots and parsnips to coat. Sprinkle with 1½ teaspoons salt and 1 teaspoon pepper and toss again. Carefully remove the preheated baking sheet from the oven and spread the carrots and parsnips over it in a single layer. Roast until the vegetables start to blister, 10 minutes.

In a separate large bowl, combine the soy sauce and remaining 1 tablespoon honey. Drizzle the mixture over the roasted vegetables and toss to coat. Sprinkle with the chopped parsley and sesame seeds.

LOBSTER BOIL

Nothing says "summer" like a giant pot of boiled lobsters—especially a pot of lobsters boiled in a stock chock-full of kielbasa, clams, corn, potatoes, fresh thyme, and beer. It's a true one-pot meal and an instant party (see Brady Boil, page 301); nothing more required than a newspaper-lined table, a great light beer, and your hands.

Serves 4 to 6

2½ pounds small
rainbow bliss potatoes

5 small yellow onions, quartered

3 medium fennel bulbs,
cut into 6 wedges and cored

1 whole garlic head,
halved lengthwise

2 (11-ounce) bottles lager beer

2 tablespoons kosher salt

1 pound kielbasa sausage,
cut on an angle into 1-inch pieces

12 sprigs fresh thyme

6 ears yellow corn,
husks and silks removed

4 (1½-pound) fresh live lobsters

2½ pounds fresh littleneck
or Manila clams

Melted unsalted butter, for serving

Lemon wedges, for serving

Crusty bread, for serving

Combine the potatoes, onions, fennel, and garlic in a large pot. Add the beer and 4 cups water. Season with the salt. Add the sausage and 5 sprigs of the thyme. Bring to a boil over high heat, then reduce the heat to medium-high. Cover and cook for 15 minutes.

Add the corn, lobsters, and remaining 7 sprigs thyme to the pot. Cover and cook for 8 minutes more. Add the clams and cook until the lobsters are bright red, the clams have opened, and the potatoes are fork-tender, an additional 7 minutes. Discard any clams that have not opened. Strain the broth from the pot for grit, and reserve.

Pour the lobster, clams, sausage, potatoes, and corn onto a table covered with newspaper. Enjoy with melted butter, lemon wedges, crusty bread, and the reserved broth.

SPICY PORK TENDERLOIN WITH SUN-DRIED TOMATO & FENNEL STUFFING

Pork is one of my favorite meats to cook with when I want something that takes on other flavors really well. It truly is the other white meat! Pork tenderloin in particular has such great, tender texture and goes really nicely with just about any glaze or rub—or, in this case, both! First I give the meat its spa moment with a cumin–cinnamon–chili powder rub-down, then it gets a quick sear before being slathered with a brown sugar, garlic, and Sriracha glaze that does double-duty as a sauce. Last, I pop it back in the pan so it caramelizes on the outside, and all those amazing pan drippings get drizzled over the top of the sliced pork along with the syrupy glaze.

Serves 4

1 teaspoon ground cumin

1 teaspoon ground cinnamon

1 teaspoon chili powder

1 teaspoon kosher salt

1 teaspoon freshly ground black pepper

1½ pounds pork tenderloin

Extra-virgin olive oil

1 cup packed light brown sugar

2 tablespoons minced garlic

1 tablespoon Sriracha

Sun-Dried Tomato & Fennel Stuffing (recipe follows)

In a medium bowl, whisk together the cumin, cinnamon, chili powder, salt, and pepper. Massage the tenderloin with the spice mixture, wrap tightly with plastic wrap, and refrigerate for 1 hour.

Preheat the oven to 350°F.

In a large cast-iron skillet or sauté pan, heat 2 tablespoons olive oil over medium-high heat. Unwrap the tenderloin and place it in the skillet. Sear for 3 to 4 minutes on each side and remove from the heat.

In a medium bowl, combine the brown sugar, garlic, and Sriracha. Use a brush to evenly glaze the tenderloin with half the sugar mixture.

Put the other half of the sugar mixture in a small saucepan and add 1 tablespoon water. Heat over medium heat, stirring occasionally, until the mixture comes to a simmer and is syrupy in consistency, about 5 minutes. Set aside.

Return the tenderloin to the pan, transfer to the oven, and bake for 20 minutes, or until a meat thermometer inserted into the center registers 140°F. Remove and let rest for 5 minutes before slicing. Pour the pan drippings over the tenderloin and serve with the glaze and the Sun-Dried Tomato & Fennel Stuffing on the side.

(Continued)

SUN-DRIED TOMATO & FENNEL STUFFING

I love fennel—I mean *love* fennel. I'm crazy about how herbaceous and fresh it is raw and how mild and sweet it gets when it's cooked down. It's a particularly nice surprise in a stuffing, where most people are expecting to find blah celery. It also plays up the subtle sweetness of the sun-dried tomatoes here, which otherwise give this dish deep, earthy flavor. This stuffing is the perfect addition to a holiday table, or with pretty much any meat dish. It's also completely vegetarian if you use vegetable broth. I call for making croutons from scratch, but you could totally buy them ready-made from the store and call it a day.

Serves 4 to 6

8 tablespoons (1 stick) unsalted butter, plus more for greasing

2 loaves white or sourdough bread, crusts removed, cut into 1-inch cubes

4 fennel bulbs, cored and coarsely chopped, fronds chopped and reserved for garnish

2 cups chicken broth

1 cup chopped drained oil-packed sun-dried tomatoes

2 tablespoons balsamic vinegar

1 teaspoon dried oregano

1 teaspoon kosher salt

½ teaspoon freshly ground black pepper

Preheat the oven to 350°F. Grease a 9-by-13-inch baking dish with butter.

Spread the bread cubes in a single layer on a large baking sheet and toast in the oven, tossing once or twice, until lightly golden, 10 to 15 minutes.

Melt the butter in a large saucepan over medium heat. Reserve 2 tablespoons of the melted butter and set aside. Add the fennel to the saucepan and cook, stirring occasionally, until tender, 20 to 25 minutes.

In a medium saucepot, combine the broth, sun-dried tomatoes, vinegar, oregano, salt, and pepper. Bring to a simmer over medium-high heat and cook for 10 minutes.

In a large bowl, toss the toasted bread with the fennel and broth mixtures, making sure the bread fully absorbs the liquid. Place the stuffing in the prepared baking dish, cover with foil, and bake for 20 minutes. Uncover the stuffing and brush it with the reserved 2 tablespoons melted butter. Bake, uncovered, until browned on top, another 20 minutes.

Garnish with the fennel fronds and serve hot.

BRADY'S FAVORITE SHORT-RIB ENCHILADAS

I will never forget one of the first dates I went on with Brady. We went to the Mexican restaurant down the street from where I was living and he ordered the enchiladas with rice and beans, and then a side of flour tortillas. *Hmm, interesting.* What he then did—and what I still make fun of him for to this day—was take his enchiladas and rice and beans, mash them together like some kind of casserole, scoop up the sloppy mess into one of the tortillas, and roll it into some kind of mutant burrito. I mean, you can take the boy out of Houston . . . But what we can agree on—being that I'm from Southern California and he's from Texas—is that good Mexican food is pretty hard to beat. Even though we may not see eye to eye on who has the best offerings (ahem, California), and even though I say real cheese and he says Velveeta, we both love a good piping-hot dish full of enchiladas. For an extra-special treat, I'll braise up a batch of short ribs to throw in the mix as one concession that those Texans know what they're talking about when it comes to tasty food.

There are two ways I like to make enchiladas: either rolling them up individually and lining them up in a dish or—and this one always blows people's minds—layering the tortillas flat with the filling ingredients like a lasagna. Either way, frying the tortillas first makes a world of difference in the flavor and texture of the final dish. You can't argue with tradition!

Serves 4 to 6

2½ pounds bone-in beef short ribs

Kosher salt and freshly ground black pepper

2 tablespoons vegetable oil, plus ½ cup for frying

1 large yellow onion, chopped

1 large fresh poblano pepper, seeded and cut into ¼-inch pieces

6 garlic cloves, minced

1 tablespoon chili powder

2 teaspoons ground cumin

1 teaspoon smoked paprika

¾ cup silver tequila

1 cup beef broth

1 (28-ounce) can red enchilada sauce (I like Las Palmas)

18 yellow corn tortillas

6 cups shredded Mexican blend cheese (about 1 pound)

½ cup crumbled cotija cheese, for serving

Crema or sour cream, for serving

Fresh cilantro leaves, for serving

(Continued)

Season the ribs generously with salt and pepper.

In a large skillet, heat the vegetable oil over medium-high heat. Add the short ribs in batches and cook until nicely browned, 2 to 3 minutes per side. Set aside.

Reduce the heat to medium. Add the onion and poblano to the pan and cook, stirring, until soft, 3 to 5 minutes. Add the garlic and cook, stirring, until fragrant, about 1 minute. Add the chili powder, cumin, and paprika and cook, stirring to make sure they're well coated with oil, until fragrant, 2 to 3 minutes. Add the tequila and use a spoon to scrape up the bits stuck to the bottom of the pan. Let the liquid boil until almost completely evaporated. Remove the pan from the heat and transfer the contents of the pan to a slow cooker.

Layer the short ribs on top of the onion mixture in the slow cooker, then add the broth. Cover and cook on Low for 8 hours, or until the meat is falling off the bones.

Preheat the oven to 375°F. Lightly oil a 9-by-13-inch baking dish.

Remove the cooked short ribs from the slow cooker and transfer them to a large plate. When cool enough to handle, remove and discard the bones, visible fat, and connective tissue. Shred the meat using your fingers or two forks and set aside.

Strain the sauce from the slow cooker through a fine-mesh strainer into a medium bowl. Use the back of a ladle to squeeze the liquid from the solids, then add the solids to the shredded meat. Stir to combine. Skim as much fat as possible from the liquid in the bowl.

In a separate medium bowl, stir together the enchilada sauce and ½ cup of the cooking liquid.

Heat the remaining oil in a large pan over medium-high heat. When the oil shimmers, add a tortilla and fry for 10 to 20 seconds on each side until just lightly browned. Transfer to a paper towel–lined plate and repeat with the remaining tortillas, layering paper towels in between.

To assemble the enchiladas, ladle about 1½ cups of the enchilada sauce over the bottom of the prepared baking dish. Add a layer of 6 tortillas to completely cover the bottom of the dish (it's okay if the edges curl up the sides). Top the tortillas with half the shredded meat and 2 cups of the Mexican cheese. Add another layer of 6 tortillas, this time trimming the edges so the tortillas sit flat in the dish. Top with another 1½ cups of the enchilada sauce, the remaining shredded meat, and another 2 cups of the Mexican cheese. Finish with the remaining 6 tortillas, 1½ cups enchilada sauce, and 2 cups Mexican cheese.

Cover with foil and bake for 20 to 25 minutes, until the cheese is bubbling. Remove the foil and bake for another 5 to 10 minutes, until the top is golden. Let cool for 5 to 10 minutes.

Serve with the cotija, a drizzle of crema and a sprinkle of cilantro leaves.

CAULIFLOWER "CHORIZO" TACOS WITH CUBAN-STYLE BLACK BEANS

One day on the set of an ad campaign I was shooting, the caterer had put out a selection of tacos—carnitas, shredded chicken, the usual suspects. But then there was a cauliflower option. It smelled amazing and tasted incredible—like nothing I'd ever had—and it was filling without feeling too heavy or starchy. So I sort of dissected it and then played around with different ingredients to figure out how to re-create it. I discovered that by tossing the cauliflower florets with sweet paprika and cumin and roasting it in a little coconut oil, I was essentially making "chorizo"—complete with the signature orange color. I layered it with Cuban-Style Black Beans, Pickled Onions, and a drizzle of Avocado Crema—almost like a thinner, tangier guacamole—and then put it to the ultimate test: serving it to Brady. Sure enough, it got the official stamp of approval.

I highly recommend including these in the spread the next time you do taco night for your family or friends, and not just because they're vegan—they're also insanely delicious.

Serves 4 to 6

FOR THE CAULIFLOWER "CHORIZO":

3 small heads cauliflower
(I like using the multicolor variety),
cut into bite-size florets

3 tablespoons coconut oil, melted

Kosher salt

1 teaspoon granulated garlic

1 teaspoon ground sumac
or lemon pepper

¾ teaspoon sweet paprika

¾ teaspoon dried thyme

½ teaspoon ground cumin

¼ cup vegetable oil

2 tablespoons grated lemon zest

FOR THE AVOCADO CREMA:

1 ripe medium avocado

¼ cup coarsely chopped
fresh cilantro

¼ cup crema or sour cream

2 tablespoons fresh lime juice
(from about 2 limes)

½ teaspoon kosher salt

¼ teaspoon ground cumin

FOR SERVING:

12 yellow corn tortillas

Pickled Onions (recipe follows)

Cuban-Style Black Beans
(recipe follows)

(Continued)

For the cauliflower "chorizo": Preheat the oven to 400°F. Line two baking sheets with parchment paper.

Divide the cauliflower florets evenly between the two baking sheets and spread them into a single layer. Drizzle the cauliflower with the melted coconut oil, season with salt, and toss to coat. Roast for 30 to 40 minutes, or until the cauliflower is tender and browned, rotating the pan halfway through.

In a small bowl, mix together the granulated garlic, sumac, paprika, thyme, cumin, and ½ teaspoon salt.

In a small skillet, heat the vegetable oil and lemon zest over medium-low heat. Stir in the dried spices and cook, stirring, until fragrant and toasted, 2 to 3 minutes. Remove from the heat. Drizzle the seasoned lemon oil over the baked cauliflower and toss to coat. Return to the oven for another 10 minutes.

For the avocado crema: Use a spoon to scoop the avocado flesh into a food processor. Add the cilantro, crema, lime juice, salt, and cumin and process until smooth.

To assemble: Wrap the tortillas in foil and warm them in the oven for 15 to 20 minutes. Lay a tortilla on a plate and add a spoonful of the cauliflower, a dollop of avocado crema, and a heap of Pickled Onions. Repeat with the remaining tortillas and serve with the Cuban-Style Black Beans.

PICKLED ONIONS

These are super-quick to make, last forever in the fridge (okay, a month, but that's pretty good!), and add the perfect bright note to just about anything.

Makes 2 cups

1 cup rice vinegar

¼ cup sherry vinegar

2 tablespoons agave nectar

⅛ teaspoon ground cumin

½ teaspoon kosher salt

4 small red onions, thinly sliced

In a medium saucepan, combine the vinegars, agave, cumin, and salt and bring to a boil over medium heat.

Place the sliced onions in a heatproof bowl and pour the hot pickling liquid over them. Make sure the onions are completely submerged and let them steep until they cool to room temperature. Refrigerate until chilled, about 1 hour. These will keep in an airtight container in the fridge for up to 1 month.

CUBAN-STYLE BLACK BEANS

I wish I could say this recipe was totally and completely mine, but it's actually an old ex-boyfriend's mother's. She personally taught me how to make these, which was incredible because she barely spoke any English; I had to learn by watching exactly what she did. I then taught my mom how to make them, and we've both been making them ever since. The recipe stayed; the boyfriend didn't.

This dish is a labor of love. You soak the beans for a few hours and simmer them for two—but they have so much flavor and body that you could just put them over rice and call it a frickin' meal.

Makes about 6 cups

1 pound dried black beans, rinsed, drained, and picked through

¼ teaspoon baking soda

1 bunch fresh cilantro

1 yellow onion, finely diced

3 bay leaves

1 teaspoon ground cumin

1 teaspoon ground oregano

1 teaspoon distilled white vinegar

1 teaspoon sugar

1 to 2 teaspoons extra-virgin olive oil

2 teaspoons kosher salt, plus more to taste

Freshly ground black pepper

In a large bowl or pot, combine the beans with the baking soda and 10 cups water and let soak for about 3 hours. Rinse and drain.

Cut or tear the stems from the bunch of cilantro. Reserve the leaves and use kitchen twine to make a bundle of the stems.

In a large stockpot, combine the cilantro stem bundle, soaked beans, onion, bay leaves, cumin, oregano, vinegar, sugar, olive oil, salt, and 10 cups water. Bring to a simmer over medium heat and cook until the beans are soft, about 2 hours. Discard the cilantro bundle and season with salt and pepper. Garnish with the cilantro leaves and serve immediately.

CHICKEN & DUMPLINGS

If I had to rank my top twenty meals of all time, Chicken & Dumplings would 100 percent be on that list. Ever since I first visited the South for beauty pageants when I was little, and then met my best friend in the world, who is from South Carolina, I kind of felt like maybe there was a little part of me that was from the South in spirit. Luckily, this dish puts the Southern in Southern California.

Chicken & Dumplings pretty much defines stick-to-the-ribs (as my mom would say) soul food. First you caramelize the chicken thighs, then simmer them until they're falling-off-the-bone tender in a broth that's been deeply flavored with browned bits from the chicken, onions, and garlic, plus parsnip, carrots, and fennel for some sweet earthiness, and just a touch of sherry—as a nontraditional twist—for just the right amount of richness. And dolloped on top are the most tender, scrumptious dumplings that I brighten up with some fresh herbs. As a good friend said when she ate a version of this on my show, they're like little "stuffing balls."

This isn't a super-quick meal to pull together, but on the day when you have time to go the extra mile, you can start this in the morning and be done by dinner. Or you could make the stew one day and make the biscuits the next.

Serves 6

FOR THE STEW:

3½ pounds bone-in, skin-on chicken thighs

Kosher salt and freshly ground black pepper

2 tablespoons vegetable oil

4 tablespoons (½ stick) unsalted butter, at room temperature

1 large yellow onion, finely diced

2 medium carrots, sliced into ¼-inch-thick coins

1 small fennel bulb, quartered, cored, and sliced into ¼-inch-thick slices

1 parsnip, peeled and sliced into ¼-inch-thick coins

2 garlic cloves, minced

½ cup plus 2 tablespoons all-purpose flour

½ cup dry sherry

4½ cups chicken broth

4 sprigs fresh thyme

For the stew: Pat the chicken dry with paper towels and season with salt and pepper.

In a Dutch oven or large pot, heat the vegetable oil over medium-high heat. Add half of the chicken and cook until golden brown, about 5 minutes per side. Transfer to a plate and repeat with the remaining chicken. Set aside to cool on a baking sheet.

In the same pot, melt the butter over medium-high heat. Add the onion and ½ teaspoon salt and cook, stirring, until soft, about 5 minutes. Add the carrots, fennel, and parsnip and cook, stirring, until just tender, 4 to 5 minutes. Add the garlic and cook, stirring, until fragrant, about 1 minute. Add the flour and cook, stirring continuously, for 2 to 3 minutes. Pour in the sherry and stir as you scrape up any bits stuck to the pan. Stir in the broth to combine.

Tie the thyme, bay leaves, and parsley together with kitchen twine and drop the bundle into the broth. Add the chicken, fully immersing it in the liquid. Bring the stew to a boil. Reduce the heat to low and cover the pot with a lid. Simmer until the chicken is fully cooked, about 1 hour. Remove from the heat.

(Continued)

2 bay leaves

3 or 4 sprigs fresh flat-leaf parsley

FOR THE DUMPLINGS:

2 cups all-purpose flour

1 tablespoon baking powder

½ teaspoon baking soda

¾ teaspoon kosher salt

¼ teaspoon freshly ground black pepper

¾ cup buttermilk

6 tablespoons (¾ stick) unsalted butter, melted

2 tablespoons finely chopped fresh thyme leaves

1 tablespoon finely chopped fresh flat-leaf parsley leaves

1 tablespoon finely chopped fresh dill

Remove the bundle of herbs from the pot and discard. Remove the chicken and transfer it to a cutting board. When the chicken is cool enough to handle, remove and discard the skin and bones. Tear the meat into bite-size pieces. Using a skimmer or wide spoon, skim the fat from the surface of the stew in the pot. Return the chicken and any drippings that have collected on the cutting board to the stew. Bring the stew to a simmer.

For the dumplings: In a medium bowl, whisk together the flour, baking powder, baking soda, salt, and pepper. Add the buttermilk, butter, thyme, parsley, and dill and stir to form a thick and very sticky dough.

On a lightly floured work surface, use your hands to roll the dough into golf ball–size balls. Drop the dough balls into the simmering stew, spacing them about ¼ inch apart. Cover and simmer over low heat until the dumplings are firm and cooked through, about 15 minutes. Serve hot.

WHOLE GRILLED TROUT

Growing up, I spent every summer in the Sequoia Mountains in California, where my grandparents had a cabin. My grandfather taught me to fish, and at first I wasn't crazy about it—namely because his rule was "you catch it, you clean it," so I dreaded having to actually do that. I remember the first time I cleaned a fish like it was yesterday. It was the most beautiful rainbow trout, and after I managed to scrape out all the guts, we stuffed the fish with lemon and put it on the grill. It was, quite possibly, the most delicious meal I've ever eaten. This recipe honors that true simplicity, adding only fresh herbs, because it really is all about the fish. It's also the most impressive presentation that still manages to feel homey and rustic.

Serves 4 to 6

4 whole trout
(about 1 pound each), gutted,
scaled, rinsed, and patted dry

Kosher salt and freshly
ground black pepper

3 lemons:
1 sliced and 2 halved

8 sprigs fresh dill

8 sprigs fresh flat-leaf parsley

8 sprigs fresh tarragon

Vegetable oil,
for brushing the grill

Charred Wedge Salad with
Greek Yogurt Blue Cheese Dressing
(recipe follows)

Heat a grill to medium-high.

Season the cavity and the outside of each trout with salt and pepper. Line each cavity with lemon slices and fill with 2 sprigs each of dill, parsley, and tarragon. Close the cavity, folding one side of the trout over the other. Tie the trout with kitchen twine in several places to make sure that the herbs and lemon slices are secured inside.

Rub the grill grates with vegetable oil and lightly oil a grill basket large enough to fit the fish. Place the fish in the basket and grill on one side until lightly charred, 7 to 8 minutes. Flip the basket and continue to cook the fish until the flesh is opaque and lightly charred, 6 to 8 minutes. While the second side cooks, add the halved lemon to the grill cut-side down and cook until charred, about 6 minutes.

Gently remove the fish from the basket and cut the strings. Transfer to a serving platter and serve each fish with a grilled lemon half. Serve with the Charred Wedge Salad with Greek Yogurt Blue Cheese Dressing.

(Continued)

CHARRED WEDGE SALAD WITH GREEK YOGURT BLUE CHEESE DRESSING

Whenever I have the grill going for dinner, I'm always thinking about what else I can throw on there. There's veggies, of course, and fruit, but then I started wondering about salad. I discovered that romaine in particular gets savory and smoky when it gets just kissed by the hot grill, which I play up by drizzling it with a cool yogurt dressing studded with smoky blue cheese. It's a dark and moody alternative to a usually fresh and crisp wedge salad.

Serves 6

FOR THE DRESSING:

½ cup plain whole-milk Greek yogurt

3 tablespoons buttermilk

2 tablespoons fresh lemon juice (from 1 lemon)

1 garlic clove, minced

Kosher salt and freshly ground black pepper

½ cup crumbled blue cheese

FOR THE SALAD:

2 cups cubed day-old sourdough bread

¼ cup extra-virgin olive oil

Kosher salt and freshly ground black pepper

3 heads romaine lettuce

6 bacon slices, cooked and chopped

For the dressing: In a large bowl, whisk together the yogurt, buttermilk, lemon juice, and garlic. Season with salt and pepper to taste, then fold in the blue cheese. Serve immediately or store in the fridge for up to 3 days.

For the salad: Preheat the oven to 375°F. Line a large sided baking sheet with parchment.

Spread the bread over the prepared baking sheet and toss with 2 tablespoons of the olive oil, a pinch of salt, and a few cracks of pepper. Toast in the oven for about 10 minutes, or until golden brown. Set aside to cool. When cool enough to handle, crush the croutons with a rolling pin into small bread crumbs.

Preheat the grill to medium-high heat.

Halve the romaine heads lengthwise through the root end, keeping the leaves attached. Lightly oil the romaine with the remaining 2 tablespoons of olive oil. Place the lettuce cut-side down on the grill and cook until charred and slightly wilted, 2 to 3 minutes. Transfer to a platter and season with salt and pepper. Drizzle with the dressing and garnish with the chopped bacon and bread crumbs.

LUXE BLUE CHEESE BURGER

It's pretty hard to improve on a simple ground sirloin patty and a bun, but I say if you're gonna do burgers, you gotta do *burgers*. I like layering mine up with all the heavy-hitters: caramelized onions, smoky bacon, avocado, and a big ol' dollop of Special Sauce. But the real crowd-pleaser? Stuffing the patties with blue cheese so that everyone gets a cheesy, gooey surprise.

Serves 6

6 applewood-smoked bacon slices

1 tablespoon vegetable oil, plus more for oiling the grill

2 medium white onions, cut into ¼-inch-thick half-moons

2 pounds ground sirloin

1 tablespoon Worcestershire sauce

Kosher salt and freshly ground black pepper

10 ounces mild blue cheese, chilled and cut into ½-inch cubes

6 brioche hamburger buns

Special Sauce (recipe follows)

2 Roma (plum) tomatoes, sliced

6 Boston lettuce leaves

2 avocados, thinly sliced

Preheat the oven to 400°F. Line a large rimmed baking sheet with parchment paper and set a wire rack over the pan.

Lay the bacon strips on the rack in a single layer. Cook until crisp, 20 to 25 minutes. Remove from the oven and let cool. When cool, halve each slice crosswise. Set aside.

In a large sauté pan, heat the vegetable oil over medium-high heat. Add the onions and cook, stirring frequently, until they are golden and caramelized, about 15 minutes. Set aside.

In a medium bowl, gently combine the sirloin, Worcestershire, ½ teaspoon salt, and ¼ teaspoon pepper. Divide the meat into 6 equal portions and form each into a ball. Using your thumb, gently poke a hole straight into each burger, just beyond its center. Create a small cavity and fill it with a cube of blue cheese. Close the meat around the cheese, making sure to fully seal it. Gently press the ball between your palms to flatten it into a patty, being careful not to create any openings for the cheese to escape through.

Preheat the broiler. Place the buns on a baking sheet, cut-side up. Toast the buns under the broiler until golden, 1 to 2 minutes.

Heat a grill to medium-high.

Season the outside of the burgers with salt and pepper. Lightly oil the grill grates. Working in batches, if necessary, add the burgers to the grill with enough space between them to comfortably flip. Cook the meat to medium doneness, 2 to 3 minutes on each side. Repeat until all the burgers are cooked.

(Continued)

To assemble: Spread 2 tablespoons of Special Sauce onto each bottom bun and layer with caramelized onions, a burger patty, tomato slices, a lettuce leaf, avocado slices, and 2 half slices of bacon. Top with the top of the bun slathered with more Special Sauce.

SPECIAL SAUCE

Thousand Island dressing was my all-time favorite dipping sauce as a kid. I would use it for everything—my burgers, my fries, my grilled cheese. For me, it wasn't about ketchup; it was about the dressing. This sauce is my nod to that and, of course, Big Mac sauce.

Makes about ¾ cup

½ cup mayonnaise

2 tablespoons ketchup

2 teaspoons Sriracha

2 teaspoons horseradish mustard

2 teaspoons very finely diced gherkins (about 2)

In a small bowl, whisk together the mayonnaise, ketchup, Sriracha, horseradish mustard, and gherkins. Refrigerate until ready to use, up to a week.

BEEF & MUSHROOM STROGANOFF WITH CREAMY POLENTA

My mom made beef stroganoff once a week like clockwork. Nothing against her, but I wasn't a fan. She made a totally traditional version, complete with sour cream stirred in, which—let's be honest—made it look like dog food. But even though it was a little heavy and a little weird looking, it's still a dish that brings me right back home every time I think of it.

This lighter, brighter version of the old-school classic lets you taste all the distinct layers of flavor. You have hearty sliced beef sirloin (no cubed mystery meat here!), earthy wild mushrooms and baby spinach, fresh herbs, and a brandy gravy that's silky and rich. Instead of buttered egg noodles, I serve the whole lot over creamy polenta and dollop each dish with sour cream. It's the same savory, filling, yummy idea as the original—just a little more refined.

Serves 4

FOR THE POLENTA:

2½ teaspoons kosher salt

2 cups coarse cornmeal or polenta (not instant)

FOR THE STROGANOFF:

4 tablespoons extra-virgin olive oil

2 Spanish onions, thinly sliced

1 large shallot, thinly sliced

1 tablespoon minced garlic

3 sprigs fresh thyme

Kosher salt and freshly ground pepper

4 cups sliced mushrooms, such as oyster, maitake, cremini, or shiitake

12 ounces beef sirloin, thinly sliced (ask your butcher to slice it for you)

¼ cup brandy

1 cup beef broth

2 cups packed baby spinach leaves (stems trimmed)

Sour cream, for serving

Chopped fresh parsley, for garnish

Grated lemon zest, for garnish

(Continued)

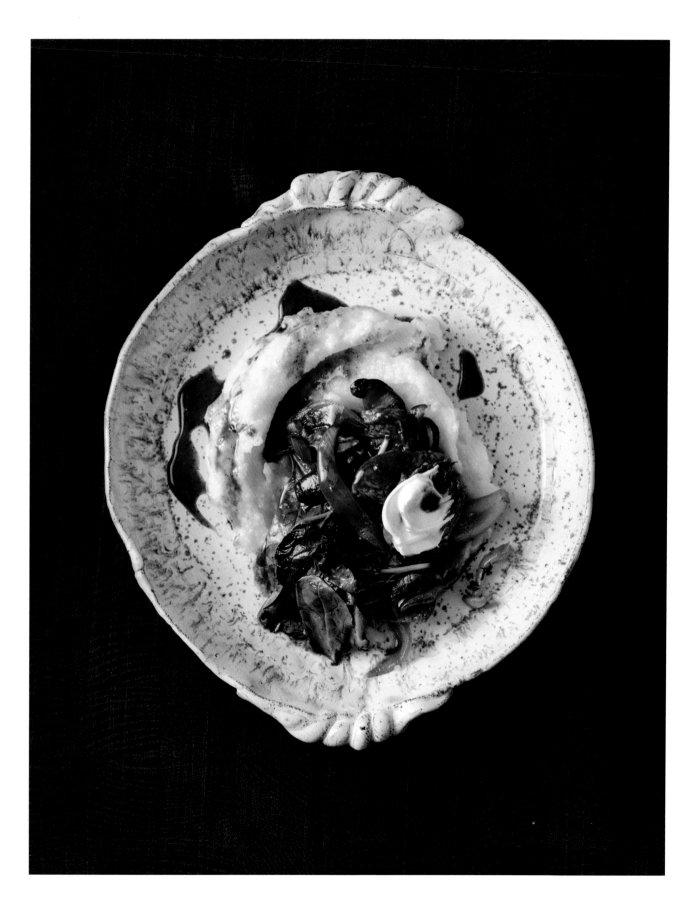

For the polenta: In a medium saucepan, heat 4½ cups water over medium heat. Add the salt and bring to a boil. Whisk in the polenta and reduce the heat to medium-low. Cook, stirring frequently to eliminate lumps and prevent burning, until the polenta is thickened and cooked through, about 15 minutes.

For the stroganoff: In a large skillet, heat 2 tablespoons of the olive oil over medium heat. Add the onions and shallot and cook, stirring, until soft, 6 to 8 minutes. Add the garlic and thyme and cook, stirring, until fragrant, about 1 minute. Season with salt and pepper. Add the mushrooms and cook, stirring, until the liquid released by the mushrooms has evaporated and the mushrooms brown, 8 to 10 minutes. Remove the thyme sprigs from the mixture and discard. Transfer the mixture to a large bowl. Set aside.

In the same skillet, heat the remaining 2 tablespoons olive oil over medium-high heat. Season the sirloin with salt and pepper and cook until browned, 1 to 2 minutes per side. Transfer to the bowl with the caramelized mushrooms.

Remove the skillet from the heat. Add the brandy, return the skillet to the heat, and use your spoon to scrape up all the bits on the bottom of the pan. Let the brandy simmer for 2 minutes. Add the broth and let it come to a simmer. Stir in the spinach and let them wilt before returning the mushrooms and meat to the pan. Cook just long enough to heat through. Adjust the seasoning with salt and pepper, if desired.

To assemble: Top the polenta with the stroganoff and serve with sour cream, parsley, and lemon zest.

PIZZA!

We eat *a lot* of pizza in our house. When I tell people that we make our own from scratch (or mostly from scratch, on occasion), they can't believe that we'd go through all that trouble. And I get it—growing up, pizza meant delivery or frozen. But if there's one thing I've learned, it's that there's nothing to making a simple dough (that keeps really well in the freezer), topping it with a bunch of delicious ingredients, baking it off, and eating it—no plates required! And there's really no wrong answer for what to put on your pizza, whether it's super-simple sauce and cheese; something a little more grown-up like broccoli rabe, prosciutto, and burrata; or light and fresh like arugula, grapes, and ricotta.

Harper especially loves pizza night because it means she can top her own—or "decorate it" as she likes to say. And it's fantastic for feeding a crowd. Check out page 302 for more ideas for hosting your own pizza party!

SPICY SAUSAGE, GARLIC KALE & GOAT CHEESE PIZZA

Serves 4

Extra-virgin olive oil

2 large Tuscan kale leaves, ribs removed, leaves torn into 1-inch pieces

1 garlic clove, minced

2 tablespoons chicken broth

Kosher salt

2 spicy sausage links, casings removed

1 ripe tomato, seeded and coarsely chopped

5 fresh basil leaves

1 cooked From-Scratch Grilled Pizza Crust (page 164)

2 tablespoons crumbled goat cheese

Preheat the oven to 400°F.

In a medium skillet, heat 1 teaspoon olive oil over medium heat. Add the kale and cook, stirring occasionally, until it just starts to wilt, 1 to 2 minutes. Add the garlic and cook, stirring, until fragrant, about 1 minute. Add the broth and cook until all the liquid has evaporated. Season with salt and set aside.

In the same skillet, heat 1 teaspoon olive oil over medium-high heat. Add the sausage and cook, breaking it up into smaller pieces with a spoon, until it fully browns, 5 to 7 minutes. Transfer the cooked sausage to a paper towel–lined plate and set aside.

In a food processor, combine the tomato, basil, 2 teaspoons olive oil, and a good pinch of salt. Pulse until combined but still slightly chunky. Add more olive oil if you'd like a thinner sauce.

Drizzle the cooked pizza crust with a little bit of olive oil. Spread the tomato sauce over the crust and top with the cooked kale, the sausage, and the goat cheese. Bake for 7 to 10 minutes, until the goat cheese starts to brown and the kale begins to char. Slice and serve hot.

BROCCOLI RABE, PROSCIUTTO & BURRATA PIZZA

Serves 4

Extra-virgin olive oil

1 bunch broccoli rabe, stems trimmed

2 garlic cloves, minced

Kosher salt

1 cooked From-Scratch Grilled Pizza Crust (page 164)

6 ounces burrata cheese

4 slices prosciutto

1 tablespoon unsalted butter

10 fresh sage leaves

¼ teaspoon red pepper flakes

Flaky sea salt, for serving

Preheat the oven to 400°F.

In a large sauté pan, heat 1 teaspoon olive oil over medium heat. Add the broccoli rabe and half the garlic and cook, stirring occasionally, just until the garlic is fragrant, 1 minute. Add ¼ cup water and a pinch of salt. Cover and cook until the broccoli rabe is bright green and tender, 6 to 8 minutes. Transfer to a paper towel–lined plate to dry.

Drizzle the cooked pizza crust with olive oil and top with the remaining garlic. Break apart the burrata and sprinkle the pieces evenly over the top of the crust. Finish with the broccoli rabe. Bake until the burrata starts to melt, 4 to 5 minutes. Drape the prosciutto slices over the pizza and return it to the oven. Bake for an additional 5 to 7 minutes, until the prosciutto is slightly crispy.

While the pizza cooks, in a small sauté pan, melt the butter over medium-high heat. Fry the sage leaves until crisp, about 30 seconds. Transfer to a paper towel–lined plate and sprinkle lightly with salt.

Sprinkle the pizza with the fried sage, red pepper flakes, and an extra pinch of sea salt. Slice and serve hot.

ARUGULA, GRAPE & RICOTTA PIZZA

Serves 4

½ cup Homemade Ricotta
(page 276) or store-bought

1 cooked From-Scratch
Grilled Pizza Crust (recipe follows)

2 cups loosely packed baby arugula

½ cup red grapes, halved

Grated zest of 1 lemon

Lemon oil, for drizzling

Flaky sea salt, for serving

Preheat the oven to 400°F.

Spread the ricotta over the cooked pizza crust. Bake until the ricotta is warmed through, about 6 minutes. Top with the arugula, grapes, and lemon zest. Drizzle with some lemon oil and season with flaky sea salt. Slice and serve hot.

FROM-SCRATCH GRILLED PIZZA CRUST

I know making dough can seem a little scary, but I promise you there's nothing to fear. Think of it as a big (delicious) science experiment, and one that's almost impossible to mess up. But if you're not convinced—or really in a pinch for time—just run to your nearest Italian market or pizza joint and buy some dough from them—no shame in that!

I do two things that give my pizza dough even more flavor: First, I use a mix of all-purpose and whole wheat flour. I love the chewy texture and subtle nutty flavor that the whole wheat flour gives it, while still very much tasting like traditional pizza dough. And second, I grill the dough, which gives it a little bit of smokiness as if it came out of a wood-fired oven, and also makes it look really pretty.

The best part about this dough, though, is that if you only use half a batch (since each batch makes two pizzas), you can freeze the other half for next week's pizza night.

Makes 2

1 (.25-ounce) packet active dry yeast

2 teaspoons sugar

¾ cup warm water

1 cup all-purpose flour

1 cup whole wheat flour

1 teaspoon kosher salt

2 tablespoons extra-virgin olive oil, plus more as needed

In a small bowl, combine the yeast, sugar, and warm water. Let sit for 10 minutes until it begins to foam.

In a large bowl, combine the flours and salt and then form a well in the center. Pour the yeast mixture and olive oil into the well. Using a fork, incorporate the wet ingredients into the dry ingredients until a dough forms.

On a lightly floured surface, knead the dough until it is smooth and elastic, about 5 minutes.

Lightly coat a clean large bowl with olive oil and add the dough, turning once to coat the dough with oil. Cover with plastic wrap or a clean kitchen towel and set the bowl in a warm place to rise until the dough has doubled in size, about 1 hour.

Preheat a grill to medium-high or a grill pan over medium-high heat.

Cut the dough in half. Place one half back in the bowl and cover, or if you're only making one pizza crust, wrap it tightly in plastic wrap and store it in the fridge or freezer. Lay the other half on a lightly floured surface. Stretch the dough into a 14-inch oval. It doesn't have to be perfect—sometimes mine have bit of a rectangular shape and sometimes they are more oval; the important thing is that you stretch the dough out so it is only about ¼ inch thick.

Place the dough on the grill. Cook until the dough is charred and grill marks form, about 1 minute per side. Transfer to a baking sheet before adding the toppings.

TIPPLES
AND
PARTY
NIBBLES

No-sweat entertaining, whether it's having four people over to watch the Grammys or fifty people for New Year's, all comes down to a few simple things: thinking about the mood you want to create, considering your guests' comfort, and a couple great recipes (done!). If I'm hosting a game night, I don't want people to have to hold a plate—because you should have cards in one hand and a drink in the other!—so I'll do lots of handheld options like Samosa Hand Pies or Curried Deviled Eggs. If it's a cocktail party, I want to make sure I put out enough food and offer enough variety that no one leaves hungry—even if I'm not technically serving a meal. That's when I pull out Spreads in Jars like Pimento Cheese, Lemon Feta, and Mushroom Pâté along with homemade breadsticks or a mega Antipasti Platter (That Nobody Will Know Is Store-Bought). Plus, by putting a little dish or board of something on surfaces throughout the house, maybe bowls of Whiskey-Glazed Nuts or Eggplant Crisps with Honey Drizzle, it keeps everyone circulating and mingling. For a more intimate gathering or something like a movie night where everyone wants to settle in and get comfy, arrange the food so that no one needs to give up their little nook to get an extra bowlful of Salted Caramel Popcorn.

As for how much food to make for a gathering, I say more is more. I'd much rather have too much than not enough. I either send people home with a doggy bag, repurpose the leftovers for meals throughout the week, or offer it up to our neighbors (or our chickens!).

When it comes to what to drink, I love offering a cocktail to guests, but there's no way I'm going to play bartender all night. That's why, in addition to a selection of beers and wine plus something sparkling, I offer one signature drink. Just like with the dishes I serve, I get inspired by looking at the classics and thinking of ways I can reinvent them—sangria, sweet tea, greyhounds, margaritas. Then I think about the theme of the night or the reason we're getting together. Is it laid-back and casual? A little more buttoned-up and polished? What season are we in? With inspiration in hand, I get to work experimenting with interesting flavor combinations and presentations, whether it's infused simple syrups, fresh herb–studded ice cubes, or putting a sophisticated cocktail into a pitcher for a more casual vibe.

No matter what kind of party you're having, don't forget that the most important thing is that you get to enjoy yourself—which means keeping (party-related) stress to a minimum. That's why many of the recipes in this chapter are meant to be mixed and matched with store-bought items, or in some cases call for simply adding ingredients to ready-made items. (Gruyère-Thyme Rolls!) Don't feel like you need to cook every single thing on the menu—so overrated! Also, don't forget about the power of the checklist. See page 290 for my tips on pulling off a party without losing your marbles.

WHISKEY-GLAZED SPICED NUTS

Little bowls of nuts are irresistible munchies, especially when cocktails are involved. These take the usually just-salty snack to a whole different place that's a little sweet, a little spicy, and a little boozy. I like to keep a batch of these in my freezer, so I have an instant snack for unexpected guests or for when a casual afternoon spent hanging around turns into an unplanned party.

Makes about 2 cups

⅔ cup raw unsalted cashews

⅔ cup raw unsalted walnuts

⅔ cup raw unsalted almonds

2 tablespoons unsalted butter

2 teaspoons whiskey

¼ cup light brown sugar

½ teaspoon coarsely chopped fresh rosemary, plus more for garnish

10 to 12 splashes of hot sauce

Flaky sea salt

Line a large baking sheet with parchment paper.

In a large nonstick skillet, combine the cashews, walnuts, and almonds. Cook over medium heat, stirring frequently, until they are just toasted, 2 to 3 minutes. Add the butter and whiskey and stir until the butter has completely melted and the nuts are coated, another 2 to 3 minutes. Stir in the brown sugar and cook until it just starts to smoke, 3 to 4 minutes. Cook, stirring the nuts to keep them from burning, until the brown sugar coats the nuts completely, 1 to 2 minutes. Remove from the heat and stir in the rosemary.

Spread the nuts over the prepared baking sheet. Drizzle with the hot sauce and sprinkle with sea salt. Toss to combine and then spread the nuts into a single layer. Let them cool.

Either garnish with fresh rosemary and serve immediately or store in an airtight container in the fridge for up to a month or the freezer for up to 3 months.

170

CHEESE BISCUIT CRACKERS

Flaky, salty, cheesy, crispy—need me to go on?

Serves 6 to 8

1 cup (2 sticks) unsalted butter, at room temperature

1½ teaspoons kosher salt

2 cups all-purpose flour

8 ounces sharp yellow cheddar cheese, grated

2 cups Rice Krispies cereal, crushed until very fine

Preheat the oven to 375°F.

In the bowl of a stand mixer fitted with the paddle attachment, whip the butter until completely smooth. Add the salt and mix to combine. Slowly add the flour and mix until completely combined. Turn off the machine and scrape down the sides of the bowl. Fold in the cheese and crushed cereal by hand until evenly combined. The mixture should have the consistency of cookie dough.

Form the dough into 1-inch balls and place on a large ungreased baking sheet, leaving 2 inches between each ball. Using the back of a fork, press down on the center of each ball until it forms a flat cracker shape. Press the fork in the opposite direction to make a crosshatch pattern. If necessary, dip the fork in hot water to keep it from sticking to the dough.

Bake the crackers for 15 to 20 minutes, until they have set but not yet turned golden brown. Let them cool completely before serving. Store in an airtight container at room temperature for up to 1 week.

SPREADS IN JARS

Honestly, I wanted to include this in the cookbook because things in little jars are *so darn cute*! But also because a trio of dips is the perfect offering for guests to graze on, whether as a predinner nosh while you finish up cooking or a light meal in its own right. Serve them with a variety of crackers and toasts, or maybe a batch of Italian Breadsticks (page 189).

PIMENTO CHEESE

I started making this classic Southern offering—known as the "caviar of the South"—for two reasons: one, I got completely hooked when I had it for the first time in South Carolina, and two, my husband totally loves it, especially on sandwiches. Normally it's just a mix of cheddar cheese, mayo, and pimentos, those little red things you find stuffed into olives. I add a little Asiago cheese to glam it up a bit, but don't get it twisted—this is one down and dirty dish, and people go nuts for it. This is an especially great dip to make a day or even two ahead because the flavors continue melding as they sit.

Makes about 3 cups

2 cups grated sharp cheddar cheese

½ cup grated asiago cheese

½ cup mayonnaise

1 (4-ounce) jar pimentos, undrained

Sliced country bread, toasted, for serving

In a medium bowl, combine the cheeses and mayonnaise.

In a mini food processor, pulse the pimentos and their juices a few times until coarsely chopped. Add to the cheese mixture, stir to combine well, and serve with toasted bread. Store in an airtight container in the fridge for 1 week.

MUSHROOM PÂTÉ

This is a fun yet elegant twist on a traditional pâté. Instead of emulsifying ground meat and fat, I cook down wild mushrooms for that same rich flavor, then add a dose of creamy cashews (so it's vegan, too). It's got a smooth, silky texture that's perfect for slathering on toast.

Makes 1½ cups

1 ounce dried porcini mushrooms

3 tablespoons unsalted butter

3 tablespoons extra-virgin olive oil

1½ cups diced yellow onions

1½ pounds mixed fresh mushrooms, such as oyster, maitake, cremini, or shiitake, stemmed and coarsely chopped

1 teaspoon fresh thyme leaves

Kosher salt and freshly ground black pepper

¼ cup dry sherry

¼ cup raw unsalted cashews, soaked in cold water for at least 1 hour or overnight

In a small pot, bring 1 cup water to a boil. Remove from the heat. Add the dried porcini mushrooms and let them soak for about 30 minutes. Drain the porcinis and finely chop. Set aside.

In a large sauté pan, melt the butter with the olive oil over medium-high heat. Add the onions and cook, stirring, until tender, 7 to 8 minutes. Add the porcinis, fresh mushrooms, thyme, and a pinch each of salt and pepper. Raise the heat to high and cook, stirring occasionally, until the fresh mushrooms have released their liquid and it has evaporated, 8 to 10 minutes. Add the sherry and cook until it has also evaporated, about 2 minutes. Remove the mixture from the heat and let it cool slightly. Reserve ⅓ cup of the mushrooms and set aside.

Place the rest of the mushroom mixture in a food processor or blender. Drain the soaked cashews, reserving the soaking water. Add the drained cashews and ¼ cup of the reserved soaking water to the mushroom mixture in the blender and blend on high. Continue to add more soaking water until the consistency is similar to hummus. Transfer the mixture to a bowl and stir in the reserved ⅓ cup mushroom mixture.

Serve warm or cold. Store in an airtight container in the fridge for 1 week.

LEMON FETA

Feta is definitely one of my top cheese choices. By whipping it with lemon, garlic, and mint, I not only get a lovely, fresh addition to toasted baguette slices or breadsticks, but also an excuse to eat feta by the spoonful.

Makes 1 cup

4 ounces feta cheese, broken into chunks

¼ cup extra-virgin olive oil, plus more for drizzling

Grated zest and juice of 1 lemon

1 garlic clove, minced

½ teaspoon freshly ground white pepper

½ cup Homemade Ricotta (page 276) or store-bought

5 fresh mint leaves, finely chopped

Combine the feta, olive oil, lemon zest, lemon juice, garlic, and white pepper in a food processor or blender and pulse until combined but still slightly chunky. Transfer the mixture to a medium bowl and fold in the ricotta.

Store in the fridge in a covered container for up to a week. When ready to serve, stir in the mint and drizzle with olive oil.

GRILLED ARTICHOKES WITH HONEY-CHILI DIPPING SAUCE

I've been eating artichokes since I was a kid because they were one of my mom's favorite things to make. She'd boil them and serve 'em up with butter and mayonnaise for dipping. Certainly nothing wrong with that, but I came up with an updated take where I grill the artichokes and serve them with aioli swirled with honey and chili sauce, which adds my favorite sweet-salty combo to the mix. This is a great starter or finger food for a party.

Serves 8 as an appetizer

4 medium artichokes

1 lemon

½ cup mayonnaise

1 tablespoon honey

1 tablespoon chili sauce
(I like Heinz)

Kosher salt and freshly ground
black pepper

Extra-virgin olive oil

Cut ½ inch off the tops of the artichokes and cut off the stems. Using kitchen shears, trim the pointy tips off the leaves. Cut each artichoke in half vertically and remove and discard the fuzzy choke (a spoon works well for this). Rub the exposed flesh with lemon to prevent it from browning.

Fill a large pot with water and bring to a boil over high heat. Fit a steaming rack over the pot and place the artichokes on the rack. Cover the pot and steam until the center of the artichoke is fork-tender, about 30 minutes. Let the artichokes cool for 15 minutes.

In a small bowl, combine the mayo, honey, chili sauce, a pinch of salt, and ¼ teaspoon black pepper. Set aside.

Preheat a grill to medium-high or a grill pan over medium-high heat. Brush the artichokes with olive oil and season with salt and pepper. Grill cut-side down until nicely charred, 4 to 5 minutes.

Serve with the dipping sauce.

SAMOSA HAND PIES WITH APPLE CHUTNEY

Samosas—crispy, golden pockets stuffed with garam masala–spiced potatoes, peas, and carrots—are the original hand pies. This recipe keeps the same Indian flavors and bundles them in a simple pastry dough—that gets deep-fried, of course. They're cute, handheld, and great for making ahead—the perfect appetizer.

Makes 24 samosas

FOR THE CRUST:

2 cups all-purpose flour, plus more as needed

Pinch of kosher salt

2 tablespoons cold unsalted butter, cut into ½-inch cubes

2 tablespoons plain whole-milk yogurt

¾ cup ice water

FOR THE FILLING:

1 tablespoon vegetable oil

1 small yellow onion, finely chopped

½ medium fennel bulb, cored and finely chopped

Kosher salt and freshly ground black pepper

2 tablespoons minced fresh garlic

2 tablespoons grated fresh ginger

½ cup brown lentils

1 medium russet potato, peeled and cut into ½-inch cubes

2 tablespoons garam masala

1 teaspoon ground turmeric

1 teaspoon ground coriander

1 to 2 cups vegetable broth

1½ cups frozen mixed carrots and peas

TO ASSEMBLE:

1 quart vegetable oil, for frying

Apple Chutney (recipe follows)

For the crust: In the bowl of a food processor, combine the flour, salt, butter, and yogurt. Process for a few seconds before adding ½ cup of the ice water. Continue processing until the dough comes together and forms a ball, adding a few more tablespoons of the ice water if necessary. Turn out the dough onto a lightly floured surface and knead by hand for about a minute. Add more flour if necessary to ensure the dough does not stick to your hands or the work surface. Shape the dough into a disk and wrap in plastic. Refrigerate for at least 30 minutes.

For the filling: In a medium saucepan, heat the vegetable oil over medium heat. Add the onion and fennel and season with a pinch each of salt and pepper. Cook, stirring, until the vegetables are soft, 3 to 5 minutes. Add the garlic and ginger and cook, stirring often, until fragrant, about 2 minutes. Add the lentils, potato, garam masala, turmeric, coriander, and enough broth to cover everything by about ½ inch. Raise the heat to high and bring to a boil. Reduce the heat to medium-low, cover, and cook until the lentils and potatoes are very soft, 45 minutes.

Add the frozen carrots and peas and cook until the liquid has been absorbed by the lentils and the lentils are fully cooked, 15 to 20 minutes. If the liquid has been absorbed but the lentils are not soft, add a small amount of the broth and cook until they are soft. If the lentils are fully cooked but there's still liquid in the pot, increase the heat and cook off the remaining liquid, stirring often so as not to burn the mixture. Season to taste and set aside to cool.

To assemble: Line a large baking sheet with parchment paper and another with paper towels.

On a lightly floured work surface, divide the dough disk into quarters.

(Continued)

Work with 1 quarter at a time, keeping the remaining quarters covered with plastic wrap. Divide each quarter into 6 equal pieces. Roll each piece into a ball and then, using a floured rolling pin, roll each ball into a 4-inch circle.

Working with 1 dough circle at a time, heap about 1½ tablespoons of the filling into the center. Brush the edge of the dough with water, then fold the dough over the filling and seal the edges by pressing with your fingers. Place the samosa on the parchment-lined baking sheet and keep covered with the plastic wrap while you fill and seal the remaining samosas.

In a heavy-bottomed pan, heat 2 to 3 inches of vegetable oil over medium-high heat to 350°F.

Using a slotted spoon or spider, gently lower a batch of samosas into the hot oil. Don't add more than will comfortably fit in a single layer, or the temperature of the oil will drop and you won't end up with nice, crispy samosas. Cook until golden brown, turning once or twice for even coloring, about 5 minutes. Transfer to the paper towel–lined baking sheet and season with salt.

Serve hot with the Apple Chutney.

APPLE CHUTNEY

Chutney is an Indian condiment that's a little sweet, a little sour, and a little spiced. It goes with both savory and sweet foods, so it would be a really tasty spread on toast, muffins, or pancakes; and also on roast or grilled pork or chicken.

Makes 1½ cups

4 Granny Smith apples, peeled, cored, and cut into 1-inch chunks

2 tablespoons fresh lemon juice (from 1 lemon)

10 garlic cloves, coarsely chopped

1 (3-inch) piece fresh ginger, peeled and coarsely chopped

½ cup apple cider vinegar

1 cup sugar

1½ teaspoons garam masala

1 teaspoon ground allspice

1 teaspoon kosher salt

½ teaspoon ground cardamom

½ teaspoon ground nutmeg

¼ teaspoon cayenne pepper

In a medium bowl, toss the apples with the lemon juice and set aside.

In a blender or the bowl of a food processor, combine the garlic, ginger, and vinegar. Blend until smooth.

Transfer the garlic mixture to a medium saucepan. Add the sugar and bring to a boil over medium-high heat. Add the garam masala, allspice, salt, cardamom, nutmeg, and cayenne. Stir to combine and cook for 2 to 3 minutes. Add the apples and cook, stirring often, until the apples soften and the liquid thickens, 15 to 20 minutes. Remove from the heat and let cool slightly before serving, or cool completely and store in the refrigerator in an airtight container for up to 1 week.

GRUYÈRE-THYME ROLLS

I came up with this recipe so that I would have a simpler-than-simple go-to during the holidays when I'm way too overextended making everything else from scratch. By kneading shredded Gruyère and fresh thyme into store-bought biscuit dough and baking up rolls in muffin tins, you end up with a deceivingly easy answer to the homemade dinner roll.

Serves 6 to 8

2 tablespoons extra-virgin olive oil, plus more for greasing

3 (12-ounce) packages refrigerated biscuits

1 cup shredded Gruyère cheese

1 tablespoon picked fresh thyme leaves

½ teaspoon onion powder

½ teaspoon garlic powder

Unsalted butter, for serving

Preheat the oven to 375°F. Lightly grease a muffin tin with olive oil.

Tear the biscuits into 1½-inch pieces. In a large bowl, combine the dough pieces with the cheese, thyme, onion powder, garlic powder, and olive oil. Mix well.

Evenly divide the seasoned dough among the prepared muffin cups. Bake for 10 to 12 minutes, until golden brown.

Remove from the tin and serve warm with butter.

CHEESY QUESO

Okay, I know "cheesy queso" is redundant, but the title works because there's really no other way to describe this rich, gooey, cheese-on-cheese-on-cheese dip. It's a (slightly) dressed-up version of the classic melted Velveeta mixed with salsa, and there's not a tailgating table that's complete without it.

Serves 6

3 tablespoons unsalted butter

3 tablespoons all-purpose flour

2½ cups whole milk, plus more if necessary

Kosher salt

1 (8-ounce) package cream cheese, cut into 4 pieces

2 cups freshly shredded low-moisture mozzarella

2 cups freshly shredded Colby Jack cheese

1 (10-ounce) can diced tomatoes and green chiles, drained

Homemade Tortilla Strips (page 201) or store-bought, for serving

Melt the butter in a large skillet over medium-high heat. Whisk in the flour and cook the roux, stirring, until it begins to bubble and turns golden brown, about 1 minute. Slowly whisk in the milk. Cook, whisking, until you no longer see any lumps of flour and the mixture begins to boil. Reduce the heat to medium and cook until the mixture is thick enough to coat the back of a spoon, about 2 minutes more. Season the sauce with salt.

Stir in the pieces of cream cheese until they are melted and the dip has a smooth consistency. Remove from the heat and stir in the shredded cheeses until completely melted and combined. Fold in the diced tomatoes and green chiles, season with salt, and adjust the consistency of the dip with another splash of milk, if necessary.

Serve immediately with tortilla strips.

SALTED CARAMEL POPCORN

A sweet-salty take on the perfect party munchie.

Serves 6

⅓ cup packed light brown sugar

4 tablespoons (½ stick)
unsalted butter

¼ cup heavy cream

1 teaspoon pure vanilla extract

20 cups unsalted popped popcorn
(½ cup plus 2 tablespoons
popcorn kernels)

1 teaspoon flaky sea salt,
plus more to taste

In a medium saucepan, combine the sugar, butter, cream, and vanilla and cook over medium heat, stirring, until the butter melts and the mixture starts to bubble, 4 to 5 minutes. Set aside to cool slightly.

Put the popcorn in an extra-large bowl. Pour some of the butter mixture over the popcorn and use two rubber spatulas to help toss and evenly coat the popcorn. Alternate pouring and tossing until you've used all the butter mixture. Sprinkle with flaky sea salt as you toss and serve immediately.

188

ITALIAN BREADSTICKS

I can't say enough great things about homemade breadsticks. You can put them out with just about anything, from cheese plates to soup and salad to Spreads in Jars (page 172)—they're easy as pie to make (actually, even easier than pie), and they almost look like art when they're arranged in a glass.

Serves 6 to 8

3 cups all-purpose or bread flour

2 teaspoons active dry yeast

2 teaspoons kosher salt

1 teaspoon sugar

Extra-virgin olive oil

½ cup semolina flour or fine yellow cornmeal

In a food processor, combine the flour, yeast, salt, and sugar. Pulse once or twice to combine. Stream in 2 tablespoons olive oil as you pulse a few more times. With the motor running, add 1 cup water through the feed tube. If necessary, continue to add water, 1 tablespoon at a time, until the mixture forms a ball. The dough should be rather sticky.

Coat a large bowl with olive oil. Add the dough to the bowl and turn to coat the dough completely with oil. Cover the bowl with plastic wrap and let the dough rise in a warm place for 1 hour, or until about doubled in size.

On a lightly floured work surface, knead the dough lightly for about 3 minutes, forcing out the air. Reshape the dough into a ball, return it to the bowl, cover, and let the dough proof in the refrigerator for several hours or overnight.

When ready to bake the breadsticks, preheat the oven to 400°F. Lightly grease a large baking sheet with olive oil and sprinkle it with the semolina.

Cut the dough into 3 equal pieces.

To roll by hand: On a well-floured surface, roll each piece of dough out as thin as possible into a large rectangle, about 8 inches long. Use a sharp knife or pastry wheel to cut the dough into roughly ¼-inch-wide strips (slightly smaller is better than bigger).

To roll with a pasta machine: Using a rolling pin, roll each piece of dough to a ¼-inch thickness. Run it through a pasta machine on the largest setting, then cut it into 12-inch-long strips.

Twist each strip as though you were wringing a washcloth, to create twisted rods. Lay them on the baking sheets and brush with olive oil. Bake until crisp and golden, 10 to 20 minutes. Cool completely before serving or storing.

The breadsticks will keep in an airtight container for up to 1 week.

BACON FAT FRIES
WITH BLUE CHEESE AIOLI

We are a houseful of bacon lovers, so when I was thinking of ways to up the ante on a normal french fry, I immediately thought of using bacon fat instead of the usual vegetable oil for frying. The result: smoky, porky flavor. It's not like biting into a piece of bacon, but it gives the fries a little extra sumpin' sumpin'. And don't think serving these is reserved for backyard hoedowns or other casual get-togethers. Stand the fries upright in jars or glasses and put dipping sauces in pretty little containers, and you have a sophisticated dipping station. I like to include a spicy ketchup (just a little store-bought ketchup mixed with Sriracha) and some creamy, salty Blue Cheese Aioli.

Save up all your bacon drippings to make these. Bacon fat lasts pretty much forever in the fridge, but you can also find it at some specialty grocery stores. I also call for adding some grapeseed oil, which will help stretch your bacon fat.

Serves 4 to 6

3 pounds russet potatoes

3 cups rendered bacon fat, for frying

1 cup grapeseed oil or other high-smoke-point oil, for frying

Flaky sea salt

Blue Cheese Aioli (recipe follows), for serving

Slice the unpeeled potatoes into ¼-inch-thick fry-size sticks. Submerge the potatoes in cold water until ready to use. (This will keep them from discoloring.)

Pour the bacon fat and oil into a medium pot or high-sided skillet. The oil should come about halfway up the pan. If you need to add more fat to get there, keep a ratio of 3 parts rendered bacon fat to 1 part grapeseed oil. Heat the oil to 325°F over medium-high heat. Line a large plate or baking sheet with paper towels.

Drain the potatoes and blot them dry with paper towels. Working in batches, gently lower the potatoes into the oil, being careful not to overcrowd the pan (which will lower the oil temperature and lead to soggy fries). Cook until lightly golden, 5 to 7 minutes. Use a slotted spoon or metal spider to transfer the fries to the paper towel–lined plate. Sprinkle with a few pinches of sea salt.

Raise the oil temperature to 350°F. Again working in batches, return the potatoes to the oil, taking care not to overcrowd the pan. Cook until deep golden brown, 2 to 3 minutes. Transfer to fresh paper towels to drain.

Serve hot with the Blue Cheese Aioli.

BLUE CHEESE AIOLI

Makes 1½ cups

1 large egg yolk

1 tablespoon fresh lemon juice
(from ½ lemon)

1 tablespoon minced garlic

1 teaspoon Dijon mustard

1 cup avocado oil

6 ounces crumbled blue cheese

Kosher salt

In a food processor, combine the egg yolk, lemon juice, garlic, mustard, and 1 tablespoon water and blend until smooth. With the blender running, slowly add the avocado oil in a thin stream until the mixture is fully emulsified. Add half the blue cheese and pulse until combined. Transfer to a small bowl and gently fold in the remaining cheese. Season with salt. Store in the refrigerator in an airtight container for up to 2 weeks.

CURRIED DEVILED EGGS

I grew up eating deviled eggs, which were a mainstay at neighborhood potlucks and barbecues in the summertime. By adding a little curry powder and cayenne to the mix, though, these have come a long way from their humble backyard roots. Don't worry, the spices aren't too in-your-face, just pleasantly complex—not to mention a gorgeous golden color.

A word to the wise: Don't use extremely fresh eggs for these. The fresher the egg, the harder it is to peel after it's been hard-boiled. I let mine "age" for a few days to ensure they're the perfect deviled-egg candidates.

Serves 6 to 8

12 large eggs,
at room temperature

6 tablespoons mayonnaise

2 tablespoons finely chopped
shallot

1 teaspoon curry powder

1 teaspoon dry mustard powder

1 teaspoon fresh lemon juice

½ teaspoon cayenne pepper

Kosher salt

Finely chopped fresh parsley,
for garnish

In a large saucepan, arrange the eggs in a single layer and cover with cold water. Bring to a boil and cook for 1 minute. Remove from the heat and let the eggs sit in the water for 15 minutes. Fill a large bowl with ice water and transfer the eggs to the ice bath. Let them cool for 10 to 15 minutes before peeling.

With a sharp knife, cut each egg in half lengthwise and carefully remove the yolks. Set the whites aside on a plate.

Pass the yolks through a potato ricer or sieve into a medium bowl. Add the mayonnaise, shallot, curry powder, mustard powder, lemon juice, and cayenne to the bowl and stir to make a smooth paste. Season with salt.

Arrange the whites, cut-side up, on a clean kitchen towel. Fit a pastry bag with a ½-inch French star tip (or cut the corner off a zip-top bag) and fill the bag with the yolk mixture. Pipe about a tablespoon-size rosette of the yolk mixture into the hollow part of each egg white.

Sprinkle with finely chopped parsley and serve.

HONEY-GINGER CHICKEN WINGS

These sticky, gooey, sweet-and-salty wings are like potato chips—you can't have just one. They're a staple at our Super Bowl parties, and they regularly make an appearance as an appetizer at barbecues, picnics, and game nights. They're usually all gone before anyone realizes they're not even fried!

Serves 6 to 8

½ cup honey
(preferably wildflower or mesquite)

¼ cup tamari or soy sauce

3 tablespoons toasted sesame oil

2 tablespoons grated fresh ginger

2 scallions, thinly sliced,
plus more for garnish

3 garlic cloves, minced

Grated zest and juice of 1 lime,
plus more zest for garnish

Kosher salt and freshly ground
black pepper

16 chicken wings
(about 4 pounds), tips removed,
drumettes and flats separated

In a medium bowl, whisk together the honey, tamari, sesame oil, ginger, scallions, garlic, lime zest, lime juice, ¼ teaspoon salt, and ¼ teaspoon pepper. Reserve ¾ cup of the mixture in the fridge.

Pour the remaining marinade into a 2-gallon zip-top bag. Add the chicken and seal the bag, pressing out as much air as possible. Massage the marinade into the wings. Refrigerate for at least 6 hours, preferably overnight. Before cooking, let the wings stand at room temperature for about 2 hours.

When ready to cook the wings, preheat the oven to 400°F. Line a large baking sheet with parchment paper.

Remove the wings from the marinade, reserving the marinade. Season the wings with salt and pepper and place them skin-side down in a single layer on a large rimmed baking sheet. Spoon some of the marinade over them; discard the remaining marinade. Bake for 20 minutes. Remove from the oven and flip the wings, basting with the pan drippings. Rotate the pan and bake for another 20 to 25 minutes, until the honey has caramelized and the skin is a dark amber color.

In a small saucepan, bring the reserved ¾ cup marinade (from the fridge) to a boil over medium-high heat. Cook until the liquid turns into a thick, syrupy glaze, about 4 minutes.

Coat the wings with the glaze, arrange them on a serving platter, and garnish with scallions and lime zest.

EGGPLANT CRISPS WITH ROSEMARY-INFUSED HONEY DRIZZLE

This recipe is for when you want to step up your chips-and-dip game. It scratches that same salty, crunchy itch with a little more exotic flavor and polish thanks to the naturally sweet flavor of caramelized eggplant and the rosemary-infused honey. Feel free to experiment with other flavors—any dried spice or herb will work. Thyme, tarragon, and lavender are my favorites.

Serves 4 to 6 as an appetizer

FOR THE ROSEMARY-INFUSED HONEY DRIZZLE:

2 tablespoons dried rosemary leaves

1 cup honey

FOR THE CRISPY EGGPLANT:

4 medium Italian or Japanese eggplants, sliced into ⅛-inch-thick rounds

2 cups whole milk

Vegetable oil, for frying

1 cup all-purpose flour

Kosher salt

For the rosemary-infused honey drizzle: Place the rosemary in the bottom of a clean, dry jar and pour the honey over it. Stir the honey and rosemary to fully combine. Cover the jar tightly and let the rosemary infuse for about 5 days at room temperature, turning the jar every so often so the herbs redistribute. The longer you let the herbs infuse, the more intense the flavor will be.

For the crispy eggplant: Place the eggplant slices in a large bowl and pour the milk over to cover. Use a heavy plate or bowl to weigh down the eggplant and keep it submerged. Cover with plastic wrap and let the eggplant soak in the refrigerator for at least 1 hour or up to overnight.

Drain the eggplant and let it sit at room temperature for 1 hour before cooking.

Line a baking sheet with parchment paper and place a wire rack on top.

Fill a large pan with about 1 inch of vegetable oil. Heat the oil to 350°F over medium-high heat.

Spread the flour in a shallow bowl and dredge each slice of eggplant in the flour. Take care to fully coat both sides and tap off any excess. Working in batches, carefully slide the dredged eggplant slices into the hot oil without overcrowding the pan (or the oil temperature will drop and your eggplant will be soggy). Fry the eggplant until golden brown, 2 to 3 minutes per side. Transfer to the wire rack to drain. Immediately sprinkle with salt and drizzle with the rosemary honey. Repeat with the remaining slices. Serve hot.

TROPICAL SALSA

By mixing exotic and sweet pineapple, watermelon, mango, and papaya with crunchy and savory cucumber, bell pepper, and onion, this salsa can do double-duty as a topping for fish or chicken.

Serves 4 to 6

1 cup ½-inch-diced pineapple

1 cup ½-inch-diced seedless watermelon

½ cup ½-inch-diced mango

½ cup ½-inch-diced papaya

½ cup ½-inch-diced English or other seedless cucumber

½ cup ½-inch-diced red bell pepper

1 small jalapeño, seeded and finely chopped

½ small red onion, finely chopped

½ cup chopped fresh cilantro leaves

2 tablespoons fresh lime juice (from 1 or 2 limes)

½ teaspoon chili powder

½ teaspoon kosher salt

Homemade Tortilla Chips (page 201) or store-bought, for serving

In a large bowl, mix together all the ingredients except for the chips. Let the mixture sit for at least 10 minutes to allow the flavors to blend. Serve with chips.

CLASSIC GUACAMOLE

Avocados are one of my top five foods, so it's a good thing I live in the avocado capital of the world! And my kids know a good thing too—they've both been eating full-on guacamole since they were nine months old. I keep things pretty traditional with tomato, red onion, jalapeño, cilantro, and lime juice; then I kick it up with chili powder and cotija cheese, which is like the Mexican version of feta and adds an extra layer of creamy with a hint of salty.

Serves 6 to 8 as an appetizer

6 ripe avocados
(I like Hass or Reed)

1 small red onion, finely chopped

1 large jalapeño, seeded and minced

½ cup chopped fresh cilantro leaves

½ cup crumbled cotija cheese

6 tablespoons fresh lime juice
(from about 3 limes)

2 teaspoons kosher salt,
plus more to taste

1 teaspoon chili powder

Freshly ground black pepper

Homemade Tortilla Chips
(page 201) or store-bought,
for serving

Halve the avocados, remove the pits, and scoop the flesh into a medium bowl. Add the onion, jalapeño, cilantro, cotija, lime juice, salt, and chili powder. Use a potato masher or the back of a fork to break down the avocado and incorporate the ingredients, mashing the guacamole to your desired texture. Season with more salt, if desired, and black pepper.

Serve with Homemade Tortilla Chips. This is best eaten right away, but can be stored in the refrigerator with plastic wrap pressed directly against the surface to prevent oxidizing for an hour or two.

PULL UP A CHAIR

HOMEMADE TORTILLA CHIPS

If you have the time, making your own tortilla chips is such a win. They taste so much fresher than anything out of a bag and are surprisingly easy to make. They're just corn tortillas that are baked until golden and crisp! No need to make your own tortillas, though. I'm not *that* crazy. If you're planning to serve these with soup, chili, salad, or anything else that calls for scooping, you could cut them into strips instead of triangles.

Serves 6 to 8 as an appetizer

12 corn tortillas

3 tablespoons vegetable oil

Kosher salt

Preheat the oven to 400°F. Line two large rimmed baking sheets with parchment paper.

Lay 6 tortillas on a cutting board and brush each with a light layer of the oil, making sure the edges also get coated. Sprinkle with a generous pinch of salt, then turn them over and brush the second side with oil. Stack the tortillas into a pile and cut them into 6 equal wedges or ½-inch-wide strips.

Arrange the tortillas on the prepared baking sheets in a single layer. Bake for 20 to 25 minutes, rotating the pan halfway through cooking. Once the chips are golden brown and crispy, remove them from the oven and let them cool completely. Transfer the cooled chips to an airtight container or eat immediately, which is what happens at my house.

ANTIPASTI PLATTER (NO ONE WILL KNOW IT'S STORE-BOUGHT!)

A beautifully curated antipasti platter is one of the best secret weapons you can have when it comes to feeding a crowd. Not only can you create something so gorgeous that it could be part of the décor, but it's also a great way to fill up guests without having to cook a four-course meal. Whenever I have too much on my plate and there are a bunch of people coming over for a party, I'll put together a platter—plus a signature cocktail and some wine and beer—and call it dinner. And the best part? You can make an impressive spread using entirely store-bought elements—though I do always like to try to make at least one thing myself. That said, taking the time to make it an elegant presentation and tailoring it to your guests' tastes is just as special as preparing something from scratch.

Building an antipasti platter should be all about creativity and featuring the things you love. Here are some of my favorite elements to include:

Spreads: Anything creamy, rich, salty, or sweet that plays off the other ingredients. Try Lemon Feta (page 177), Mushroom Pâté (page 175), or Tomato Jam (page 9).

Cured Meats and Cheeses: Aim for 3 or 4 of each so there's something for everyone—stinky, spicy, mild, etc. For an instant conversation starter, pick one region in the world and explore all the varieties that come from there.

Crackers and Breads: Throw in a fresh baguette and a variety of crackers or Breadsticks (page 189) for spreading and sampling.

Pickled and Cured Bits: Olives, peppers, cornichons, green beans—anything with salty, briny goodness. One of my favorite elements to play with is vegetables *sott'olio*, or veggies that have been cured and preserved "under oil." Try mushrooms, artichokes, eggplant, tomatoes, or even asparagus that have been prepared this way. You can find jars of them in most grocery stores.

Raw Bar: I love offering a twist on the traditional meat-and-cheese selection by including things like oysters and shrimp, complete with dipping options like an easy mignonette or a spicy cocktail sauce.

Fresh Fruit and Veggies: These will help balance the decadence of an antipasti platter—plus, they can look really beautiful. Figs, stone fruit, heirloom tomatoes, and radishes all look lush and appetizing when sliced and scattered or arranged whole.

Dried Fruit and Nuts: For salty and sweet textures.

HOMEMADE CHERRY SODAS

To make a party extra family-friendly—and as an option for anyone who doesn't drink alcohol—a really nice touch is offering homemade flavored sodas. You can make the flavored syrup in advance—and play around with all kinds of fruit and/or herb variations—then add the soda at the party. Major extra credit if you serve these in frosty old-fashioned bottles!

Makes 2 sodas

1 cup frozen cherries
1 cup sugar
Ice
16 ounces seltzer water
Fresh cherries, for garnish

Combine the frozen cherries and sugar in a medium pot with 1 cup water. Bring to a boil over high heat, then reduce the heat to maintain a simmer. Cook for 2 to 3 minutes, letting the sugar dissolve and the cherries defrost and soften. Pour the syrup through a fine-mesh strainer into a bowl, pressing the cherries with a spoon or spatula to release as much liquid as possible. Discard the cherries. Transfer the syrup to an airtight container and chill in the fridge.

Divide the seltzer water between two tall glasses filled with ice or chilled bottles. Add 1 tablespoon of the cherry syrup to each and stir. (Any leftover syrup can be stored in the fridge for up to 1 month.) Garnish with fresh cherries and serve with a fun straw.

HOT TODDY

My mom would make me a bourbon-free version of this classic warm cocktail whenever I'd get sick. To up the cozy factor, I've added Earl Grey tea to the mix. It still has its healing powers—especially if Mommy needs a soothing nightcap.

Serves 1

1 Earl Grey tea bag

⅓ cup hot water

2 ounces bourbon

1 tablespoon honey

1 tablespoon fresh lemon juice (from ½ lemon)

Star anise pod, for garnish

Lemon peel, for garnish

Steep the tea bag in the hot water for 5 minutes.

In a mug, combine the bourbon, honey, and lemon juice. Stir to dissolve the honey. Remove the tea bag and pour the tea over the bourbon mixture. Garnish with a star anise pod and lemon peel.

MEYER LEMON & THYME WHISKEY SOUR

This is probably the most requested cocktail in my house. It's definitely a drink that packs a punch—it'll put you under the table if you have too many—and is a really nice way to enjoy brown liquor if, like me, you're not usually inclined. Perfumed Meyer lemons—which are pretty much what you'd get if lemons and oranges had babies—plus thyme-infused simple syrup gives new, fresh life to a longtime standby. And if you really want to up the wow factor, freeze a pinch of fresh thyme in each cube of a large ice mold and use this "artisanal" ice to serve.

Serves 1

FOR THE THYME SIMPLE SYRUP:

1 cup sugar

¼ cup fresh thyme leaves

TO ASSEMBLE:

1½ ounces bourbon

1 ounce fresh Meyer lemon juice or lemon juice

Ice

Lemon peel twist, for garnish

Sprig of fresh thyme, for garnish

For the thyme simple syrup: In a medium saucepan, combine the sugar and thyme with 2 cups water. Heat over medium heat, stirring occasionally, until the sugar has dissolved, about 2 minutes. Remove from the heat and let the thyme infuse for 20 minutes. Strain the syrup and let it cool. Discard the thyme leaves. Set aside 3 tablespoons of the syrup and reserve the rest in the refrigerator for up to 2 weeks.

To assemble: Combine the bourbon, lemon juice, and reserved 3 tablespoons simple syrup in a cocktail shaker with ice. Shake well and strain into a cocktail glass over fresh ice (thyme-infused optional). Garnish with a lemon twist and a sprig of thyme. Serve immediately.

BLACKBERRY-BASIL SMASH

Like a summer garden in a glass—with a splash of bourbon, naturally.

Serves 1

FOR THE BASIL SIMPLE SYRUP:

1 cup sugar

1 cup fresh basil leaves

TO ASSEMBLE:

9 fresh blackberries, washed and dried

1 tablespoon fresh lemon juice

1½ ounces bourbon

Ice

Club soda

Fresh basil leaves, for garnish

For the basil simple syrup: In a medium saucepan, combine the sugar and basil with 2 cups water. Heat over medium heat, stirring occasionally, until the sugar has dissolved, about 2 minutes. Remove from the heat and let the basil infuse for 20 minutes. Strain the syrup and let cool; discard the basil leaves. Set aside 2 tablespoons of the syrup and reserve the rest in the refrigerator for up to 2 weeks.

To assemble: Place 6 of the blackberries in a cocktail shaker and muddle a couple of times. Add the lemon juice, reserved 2 tablespoons simple syrup, and the bourbon with ice and shake. Strain into a glass over fresh ice and top with a splash of club soda. Garnish with the basil leaves and remaining blackberries.

ROSEMARY GREYHOUND

The greyhound, a time-tested mix of grapefruit juice and vodka, is a light, bright cocktail that fits in just as perfectly at a sunny-day grill-out as it does at a holiday party. Because citrus is particularly good in the winter, though, I wanted to play up this cocktail's warm, sultry side by adding a rosemary-infused simple syrup.

Serves 1

FOR THE ROSEMARY SIMPLE SYRUP:

1 cup sugar

¼ cup fresh rosemary leaves

TO ASSEMBLE:

¾ cup ruby red grapefruit juice

2 ounces vodka

1 ruby red grapefruit slice, for garnish

For the rosemary simple syrup: In a medium saucepan, combine the sugar and rosemary with 2 cups water. Heat over medium heat, stirring occasionally, until the sugar has dissolved, about 2 minutes. Remove from the heat and let the rosemary infuse for 20 minutes. Strain the syrup and let it cool; discard the rosemary leaves. Set aside 2 tablespoons of the syrup and reserve the rest in the refrigerator for up to 2 weeks.

To assemble: Pour the grapefruit juice, vodka, and reserved 2 tablespoons simple syrup into a cocktail shaker with ice. Shake well to mix. Serve over fresh ice and garnish with a grapefruit slice.

BLUEBERRY MOJITOS

We have blueberry bushes in our yard that explode with fruit every spring, so we'll collect a heaping bowlful when the mood for anything blueberry strikes (heaping because half the berries tend to magically disappear as we cook, muddle, or bake!). No matter what I'm whipping up, I always add some lemon zest because it gives just the right amount of brightness and zip to bring out the sweetness of the berries. It works particularly well in this version of the classic Cuban highball, and the berries give it a deep, gorgeous color.

Serves 2

1 cup fresh blueberries, washed and dried, plus more for garnish

10 fresh mint leaves, plus 2 sprigs fresh mint for garnish

2 teaspoons sugar

3 limes: 2 juiced and 1 sliced into wedges

4 ounces light rum

¾ cup club soda

Ice

Muddle the blueberries in a cocktail shaker. Add the mint leaves and sugar and continue to muddle. Add the lime juice and rum and shake vigorously. Divide the club soda between two tall glasses over ice. Add the rum mixture and gently stir. Garnish with a lime wedge, a few blueberries, and a sprig of mint.

MANGO SWEET TEA

It doesn't get more Southern than a big ol' pitcher of sweet tea. There's usually not much more to it than black tea and a whole bunch of sugar, so I'm giving it a little California makeover with mango nectar and fresh mint. Splash of vodka optional!

Serves 6

4 black tea bags

1½ cups mango nectar

½ cup sugar

Ice

Fresh mint leaves, for garnish

In a medium saucepan, bring 4 cups water to a boil. Remove from the heat, add the tea bags, and steep for about 5 minutes. Discard the tea bags, then add the mango nectar and sugar. Stir until the sugar has dissolved. Set aside to cool. Pour the tea into a pitcher and refrigerate until chilled.

Serve over ice and garnish with mint leaves.

HIBISCUS SPRITZERS

For when you want a pretty pink floral twist on a simple summer sparkler.

Serves 2

4 hibiscus tea bags

2 tablespoons plus 2 teaspoons Mint Simple Syrup (page 217)

8 ounces prosecco

1 lime, sliced

In a medium saucepan, bring 3 cups water to a boil over medium-high heat. Remove from the heat and add the tea bags. Let steep for 10 minutes, then discard the teabags and let cool completely.

Pour the cooled tea and the Mint Simple Syrup into a pitcher. Stir in the prosecco. Divide between two ice-filled glasses and serve garnished with lime slices.

PINEAPPLE-SAGE MARTINI

Martinis aren't usually my first cocktail choice—I'm partial to something a little sweeter, ideally a libation that doesn't seem like you're drinking booze straight from the bottle! This version stays true to the clean flavors of a vodka martini but with a little help from fresh pineapple and earthy sage.

Serves 1

FOR THE SAGE SIMPLE SYRUP:

1 cup sugar

¼ cup fresh sage leaves

TO ASSEMBLE:

Ice

4 ounces pineapple juice

2 ounces vodka

1 sprig fresh sage, for garnish

For the sage simple syrup: In a medium saucepan, combine the sugar and sage with 2 cups water. Heat over medium heat, stirring occasionally, until the sugar dissolves, about 2 minutes. Remove from the heat and let the sage infuse for 20 minutes. Strain the syrup and let cool; discard the sage. Set aside 1 ounce of the simple syrup and reserve the rest in the fridge for up to 2 weeks.

To assemble: In a cocktail shaker with ice, add the pineapple juice, vodka, and reserved 1 ounce simple syrup. Shake and strain into a martini glass. Garnish with a sprig of sage.

BOOZY DATE MILK SHAKES

One of my favorite road-trip treats is a date milk shake on the way to Palm Springs. Back in the day, the date farmers in the area needed to figure out what to do with all their extra fruit. One figured out that he could blend them up with vanilla ice cream and sell the shakes roadside. Sure enough, date shake shacks sprouted all along the highway connecting L.A. to Palm Springs, and food history was made. I've added rum for an adult version, and it's just as sweet and satisfying as the original—without the trip to the desert.

Serves 2 or 3

6 large scoops Vanilla Ice Cream (page 281) or store-bought

½ cup pitted dates

½ cup whole milk, chilled

¼ cup light rum

Dash of ground cinnamon, plus more for garnish

Whipped cream, for serving

In a blender, combine the ice cream, dates, milk, rum, and cinnamon and blend until thick and creamy. Pour into chilled milk shake glasses and top with whipped cream and a sprinkle of ground cinnamon.

WATERMELON-MINT MARGARITAS

Pureed watermelon and mint-infused simple syrup make this the perfect drink for a barbecue, or any other sunny celebration.

Serves 2

FOR THE MINT SIMPLE SYRUP:

1 cup sugar

¼ cup fresh mint leaves

TO ASSEMBLE:

Pink sea salt, for garnish

Ice

3 cups seedless watermelon, pureed

8 ounces silver tequila

½ cup fresh lime juice (from about 4 limes)

¼ cup orange liqueur

Fresh mint, for garnish

2 limes, thinly sliced, for garnish

For the mint simple syrup: In a medium saucepan, combine the sugar and mint with 2 cups water. Heat over medium heat, stirring occasionally, until the sugar dissolves, about 2 minutes. Remove from the heat and let the mint infuse for 20 minutes. Strain the syrup and let cool; discard the mint. Set aside 2 tablespoons of the simple syrup and reserve the rest in the fridge for up to 2 weeks.

To assemble: Spread pink sea salt over a small shallow plate. Rub the rims of the margarita glasses with a lime wedge and then dip them into the salt to coat.

In a cocktail shaker, combine the ice, pureed watermelon, tequila, lime juice, orange liqueur, and reserved 2 tablespoons mint simple syrup. Shake, then strain into the rimmed margarita glasses over fresh ice. Garnish with fresh mint and lime slices.

PEACH-JALAPEÑO TEXAS TEA

There are a few different teas that you'll find in the South: sweet tea, which is just what it sounds like (black tea or Lipton's with a *whole bunch* of sugar), sun tea (tea that's left out in the sun to brew), and Texas tea, which involves a splash—or six—of booze. This version of Texas tea gets a little kick in the pants from steeping the tea with jalapeño, but the heat gets balanced by peach nectar. Finish it off with a glug of your favorite tequila for a good ol' time.

Serves 4

1 small jalapeño,
seeded and sliced

5 black tea bags

¼ cup sugar

1½ cups peach nectar

¾ cup silver tequila

2 tablespoons fresh lime juice
(from about 2 limes)

1 peach, pitted and sliced,
for garnish

Ice

In a medium pot, combine the jalapeño slices with 3 cups water. Bring to a boil over medium heat. Add the tea bags and remove from the heat. Let steep for 4 minutes. Remove the tea bags and stir in the sugar until dissolved. Let cool and then remove and discard the jalapeño slices.

Pour the cooled tea, peach nectar, tequila, and lime juice into a pitcher and stir to combine. Garnish with peach slices and serve over ice.

BLOOD ORANGE–ROSÉ SANGRIA

Sangria is the perfect brunch cocktail—it's nice and light, and it's a great make-ahead. This version, with blood orange juice and rosé, tastes just as good as it looks.

Serves 4

1 (25.4-ounce) bottle rosé wine

1 cup fresh blood orange juice

½ cup orange liqueur

¼ cup simple syrup

1 lemon, cut into 8 wedges

1 lime, cut into 8 wedges

½ blood orange, cut into pinwheels

Combine all the ingredients in a large pitcher and stir. Refrigerate for at least 4 hours before enjoying.

LET THEM EAT CAKE

(AND PIE AND COOKIES AND BROWNIES AND...)

've always been the kind of girl who likes to end her meal with a little something sweet. No matter how much I'm minding my p's and q's, I always make sure there's that option on the table, whether it's a bowl of Vanilla Bean Bread Pudding with Bourbon-Caramel Sauce or peaches that have been grilled until tender and smoky and dolloped with homemade ricotta. In this chapter, you'll find some of my favorite recipes for every manner of dessert, from fresh and light to downright sinful. I've also included my rotation of cookies, brownies, and bars that can be tucked into lunches and picnic baskets. No matter how humble or over-the-top these treats, every single one of them could hold their own on just about any table, from the poshest of dinner spreads to the most casual of family nights.

Note: In all the desserts—and some sweet breakfasts—in this book, you'll notice that I call for vanilla bean paste instead of extract. There are a couple of reasons for this: It has a lovelier, more pronounced flavor, and you get all those pretty vanilla bean flecks in the finished product. I highly recommend making the switch! If extract is all you have, though, don't let that keep you from making these recipes. You could absolutely use the same amount instead of paste.

BANANA PUDDING WITH CARAMELIZED BANANAS & SPIKED WHIPPED CREAM

By now it's no secret that I love Southern food. Give me homey, sticky, sweet, and boozy, and I'm there! To make this summer backyard cookout staple even more decadent, I caramelize the bananas with a little brown sugar and butter, giving them an even richer, warmer flavor. Then I spike the whipped cream with a kiss of dark rum. It's not enough to make you tipsy, but just the right amount to add that complex, mischievous flavor. And while I recommend making the pudding from scratch, you could absolutely buy store-bought vanilla pudding and add the other homemade touches.

Present this dessert all layered up in a trifle dish or serve it parfait-style in individual glasses.

Serves 4

FOR THE PUDDING:

6 large egg yolks

½ cup granulated sugar

2 tablespoons cornstarch

¼ teaspoon kosher salt

2½ cups whole milk

2 teaspoons vanilla bean paste
(see Note, page 223)

2 tablespoons unsalted butter

FOR THE CARAMELIZED BANANAS:

½ cup firmly packed
light brown sugar

4 tablespoons (½ stick)
unsalted butter

¼ teaspoon ground cinnamon

2 tablespoons dark rum

3 bananas,
sliced into ¼-inch-thick rounds

FOR THE SPIKED WHIPPED CREAM:

1 cup heavy cream

2 tablespoons dark rum

3 tablespoons granulated sugar

TO ASSEMBLE:

2 cups crushed vanilla wafers,
plus 6 whole wafers

(Continued)

For the pudding: In a medium bowl, whisk together the egg yolks, granulated sugar, cornstarch, and salt. Set aside.

In a medium saucepan, heat the milk over medium heat. When it's just beginning to bubble around the edges of the pan, remove it from the heat and whisk a ladleful into the egg mixture. When combined, add another ladleful. Now add the rest of the milk to the eggs, whisking continuously. (It's important to not skip this step, known as tempering the eggs, because otherwise you'll end up with scrambled eggs!)

Pour the mixture back into the saucepan and whisk over medium-low heat until it thickens, about 5 minutes. Cook, whisking continuously, until it is quite thick and glossy, about 10 minutes more. The pudding should coat the back of a spoon. If you draw a line with your finger down the back of your spoon, the mark you made should remain. Remove from the heat and whisk in the vanilla and butter. Transfer the pudding to a clean bowl. Press a piece of plastic wrap directly against the surface of the pudding, taking care to cover it completely, to prevent a skin from forming. Refrigerate for at least 4 hours or up to overnight.

For the caramelized bananas: In a small saucepan, combine the brown sugar, butter, and cinnamon and cook over medium heat until bubbling, 3 to 4 minutes. Remove the pan from the heat and stir in the rum to combine. Add the banana slices, tossing to coat them completely in the caramelized sugar.

For the spiked whipped cream: In the bowl of a stand mixer fitted with the whisk attachment, beat the cream, rum, and granulated sugar on medium speed until it holds soft peaks, 3 to 5 minutes.

To assemble: Place half the crushed vanilla wafers over the bottom of a trifle dish. Spoon half the pudding over the crushed wafers, followed by an even layer of banana slices. Top with the remaining crushed wafers, reserving 1 tablespoon, followed by the rest of the pudding and then the bananas. Layer the whole wafers over the bananas and then top with the spiked whipped cream. Sprinkle with the reserved 1 tablespoon crushed wafers. Serve immediately. You can also prepare this in advance: Assemble the entire dish but do not make the whipped cream yet. Cover and hold in the fridge overnight, then make the whipped cream right before serving, and top the pudding with it.

RASPBERRY POPS

These are an easy, refreshing dessert or sweet snack that takes no time to prep. I love serving them as an adorable summery twist on the brunch staple Bellini—just add a raspberry pop to a chilled glass of bubbly, and voilà! If serving these (sans Champagne) to a younger crowd, I advise that you thread the ice pop stick through a cupcake liner to catch any drips.

Serves 6

1 pound fresh (washed and dried) or frozen raspberries

½ cup red seedless grapes

¼ cup plus 2 tablespoons powdered sugar

½ teaspoon fresh lemon juice

1 bottle Champagne, prosecco, or other sparkling wine, chilled (optional)

SPECIAL EQUIPMENT:

Six 4-ounce ice pop molds

6 ice pop sticks

In a blender or food processor, blend the raspberries, grapes, sugar, and lemon juice until smooth. Pour the mixture into six 4-ounce ice pop molds, add a stick to each, and freeze overnight or until solid. Serve each ice pop stick-up in a glass of Champagne or as is.

MOM'S CREAM CHEESE PIE

Without fail, this was the dessert that got requested at every holiday, birthday, and special event. My mom would have to make two or three as backup, just to make sure everyone got their fill. I was always the first one with both hands in the air volunteering to make this with her, and now I've become the trusted maker of the pie. While I'm known for putting a new spin on things, this is one recipe that I haven't changed one bit—it's perfect in every way. It's a cross between a cheesecake and a pie, with a tangy, creamy filling sitting in a buttery graham cracker crust. It's always on my table for celebrations and always makes me feel like I'm home.

It's also a major perk that you can make this pie a day or two ahead and refrigerate it until you're ready to serve.

Serves 6 to 8

FOR THE GRAHAM CRACKER CRUST:

1½ cups graham cracker crumbs (from 8 to 10 graham crackers)

6 tablespoons (¾ stick) unsalted butter, melted

¼ cup powdered sugar

1 teaspoon ground cinnamon

FOR THE CREAM CHEESE FILLING:

1½ (8-ounce) packages cream cheese, at room temperature

2 large eggs, at room temperature

¾ cup granulated sugar

2 teaspoons pure vanilla bean paste (see Note, page 223)

FOR THE SOUR CREAM TOPPING:

1 cup sour cream

3½ tablespoons granulated sugar

1 teaspoon pure vanilla extract

For the graham cracker crust: Preheat the oven to 350°F.

In a medium bowl, combine the graham cracker crumbs, melted butter, powdered sugar, and cinnamon. Stir until the crumbs are evenly moistened with butter. Press the mixture into the bottom and up the sides of a 9-inch pie dish and bake for 10 minutes, until the crust is set, golden, and fragrant. Transfer to a wire rack and let cool before filling. Keep the oven on.

For the cream cheese filling: In the bowl of a stand mixer fitted with the whisk attachment or in a large bowl using a handheld mixer, whisk together the cream cheese, eggs, granulated sugar, and vanilla until smooth. Carefully pour the mixture into the cooled crust. Bake for 25 to 30 minutes, until set. Keep the oven on and let the pie cool on the wire rack for 5 minutes.

For the sour cream topping: In a small bowl, combine the sour cream, granulated sugar, and vanilla and mix until smooth. Spread the topping over the pie and bake for 10 minutes. Let cool on the wire rack. Refrigerate for at least 4 to 5 hours or up to overnight, until completely chilled, before serving.

PEANUT BUTTER & CHOCOLATE BITES

We always had a batch of these in the house around the holidays, and it was almost dangerous how easy they were to make, much less pop in your mouth! They're essentially a Buckeye, a ball of creamy peanut butter wrapped in a chocolate shell. The recipe traditionally calls for paraffin wax, but I use coconut oil. It gives you a Magic Shell effect without strong coconut flavor. These are a great no-bake do-ahead dessert—all you need to do is assemble and chill them down in the fridge. You could even freeze a batch so they're ready to go whenever a party pops up.

Makes 24 bites

FOR THE PEANUT BUTTER FILLING:

1 (16-ounce) jar crunchy peanut butter

2¼ cups powdered sugar

4 tablespoons (½ stick) unsalted butter, at room temperature

1 teaspoon vanilla bean paste (see Note, page 223)

FOR THE CHOCOLATE COATING:

¼ cup coconut oil

2 cups semisweet chocolate chips

For the peanut butter filling: Line a large baking sheet with parchment paper and set aside.

In the bowl of a stand mixer fitted with the paddle attachment, combine the peanut butter, powdered sugar, butter, and vanilla and beat on medium-low speed until well combined. Form into 1-inch balls and set them on the prepared baking sheet. Refrigerate for 2 hours.

For the chocolate coating: In a glass bowl set over a pot of simmering water (the water should not reach the bottom of the bowl), combine the coconut oil and chocolate and heat, stirring continuously, until melted, smooth, and silky, 2 to 3 minutes.

To assemble: Remove the peanut butter balls from the fridge and dip them in the chocolate using a fork. Return them to the baking sheet and let them cool to set completely. Store them in the refrigerator until ready to serve, up to 24 hours. Or place them in an airtight container and freeze for up to 1 month.

CAMPFIRE S'MORES WITH HOMEMADE MARSHMALLOWS

Not a summer has gone by where I haven't built a bonfire and toasted marshmallows. Okay, so I live in California and can do it pretty much year-round, but I still feel like this is such a seasonal rite of passage. We'll have a bunch of people over, get them to gather their own marshmallow-toasting sticks, and then help them create the s'mores of their dreams. Believe me, the adults get into it as much as the kids!

I know it's hard to improve on the traditional graham-and-chocolate combo, but layering things up with sliced bananas, creamy peanut butter, homemade jam (I'm a raspberry girl), chocolate bars, and peanut butter cups is the perfectly sweet ending to a backyard cook-out.

As yummy as store-bought marshmallows are, homemade will always be superior. They have a chewier, fluffier texture; they melt better; and you can change up the basic recipe by adding food coloring or a few drops of extract like peppermint or vanilla.

Serves 4

FOR THE HOMEMADE MARSHMALLOWS:

Nonstick cooking spray

3 (.25-ounce) packets unflavored powdered gelatin (I like Knox)

2 cups granulated sugar

⅔ cup light corn syrup

¼ teaspoon kosher salt

1 tablespoon vanilla bean paste (see Note, page 223)

Powdered sugar, for dredging

FOR THE S'MORES:

8 graham crackers, split in half into squares

2 bananas, sliced (optional)

8 chocolate peanut butter cups (optional, I like Reese's)

2 chocolate bars (optional, I like Hershey's)

1½ cups strawberries, washed, dried, stemmed, and sliced (optional)

1 cup creamy peanut or almond butter (optional)

1 cup Homemade Jam (pages 9–11) or your favorite store-bought flavor (optional)

(Continued)

For the homemade marshmallows: Line a 9-inch square baking pan with plastic wrap and coat it with cooking spray.

In the bowl of a stand mixer fitted with the whisk attachment, sprinkle the gelatin over ½ cup cold water and let it sit for 10 minutes.

In a medium saucepan, combine the granulated sugar, corn syrup, and ¼ cup water and bring to a boil. Boil for 1 minute. With the mixer running on high speed, pour the boiling syrup into the mixer bowl over the gelatin. Sprinkle in the salt and beat for 12 minutes, then add the vanilla; the mixture will quadruple in volume and become very glossy.

Using a spatula, scrape the marshmallow mixture into the prepared pan and spread it evenly. Coat another piece of plastic wrap with cooking spray and use it to press the mixture into the pan. Let the marshmallow sit for a couple of hours to set.

Sprinkle the powdered sugar over a large plate. Remove the marshmallow square from the pan, discarding the plastic wrap, and dredge it in the powdered sugar. Cut the marshmallow block into 12 pieces with scissors or a knife and dredge each marshmallow in the powdered sugar once more to coat all sides. Store the marshmallows in an airtight container for 1 to 2 days.

For the s'mores: Sandwich the marshmallow squares and any variation of my suggested toppings between the graham crackers. My favorite combination is marshmallows with bananas and peanut butter cups, but you should sample them all before making any decisions!

BAKED PEARS WITH CURRANTS & CINNAMON

This is one of those deceptively simple desserts that takes almost no time to make but looks like edible art on the table. While most poached or baked pear recipes call for the pears to be peeled and cored before cooking, I like to leave mine be. It helps the pears keep their gorgeous, voluptuous shape and celebrates the natural beauty of the fruit. It's a stunning addition to a holiday table, or whenever you want something beautiful, warm, and sweet to eat. Swap out the butter for coconut oil to make it vegan.

Serves 10 to 12

6 Anjou pears, halved lengthwise

3 tablespoons sugar

1 teaspoon ground cinnamon

3 tablespoons unsalted butter, cut into ½-inch cubes, or 3 tablespoons coconut oil

¾ cup white wine

½ cup dried currants

Crème fraîche or mascarpone, for serving (optional)

Preheat the oven to 375°F.

In a shallow 2-quart baking dish, arrange the pears cut-side up. Sprinkle the pears with the sugar and cinnamon and add a small pat of butter to each pear. Carefully pour the wine into the bottom of the pan. Sprinkle the currants over the pears (it's okay if some fall into the wine). Bake the pears until they're fork-tender, about 50 minutes. Let cool for 5 to 10 minutes.

To serve, spoon the pears onto a plate and add a dollop of crème fraîche, if desired. Drizzle with some of the juices and currants from the baking pan.

TRI-BERRY TRIFLE

In the summer, food should be lighter—especially dessert. Plus, it's the time of year when the kids aren't in school, so recipes get a little bit quicker, a little bit simpler, and a little bit easier to make ahead. This dessert is the perfect answer, while still being oh-so-pretty to put out. All you have to do is layer up slices of pound cake (store-bought is completely acceptable), fluffy mounds of vanilla pudding–whipped cream, and heaps of your favorite fresh berries. ("Layers of love," as I like to call them.) A proper trifle dish isn't required, though it does add a certain something. You could easily serve this in a big glass bowl or individual jars—it's all about seeing those gorgeous layers.

Serves 6 to 8

2 cups heavy cream

1 cup whole milk

1 cup crème fraîche

1 (3.4-ounce) package instant vanilla pudding mix

2 cups fresh strawberries, washed, dried, stemmed, and sliced

1 cup fresh blueberries, washed and dried

1 cup fresh blackberries, washed and dried

1 loaf pound cake, cut into 1-inch cubes (about 6 cups)

Grated zest of 1 lemon

1 sprig fresh mint

In the bowl of a stand mixer fitted with the whisk attachment, whip the cream on high speed for 3 to 4 minutes until it holds soft peaks. Transfer the whipped cream to a separate bowl and set aside.

In the same stand mixer bowl (no need to wipe it out first), whisk together the milk, crème fraîche, and pudding mix on medium to high speed until thickened, 2 to 3 minutes. Fold in the whipped cream and set aside.

In a separate large bowl, gently combine the strawberries, blueberries, and blackberries.

Place half the cubed pound cake over the bottom of a trifle dish or large glass bowl. Arrange a third of the berries over the cake. Top with half the pudding mixture. Repeat with the remaining pound cake, another third of the berries, and the remaining pudding. Refrigerate, covered, for at least 2 hours or up to overnight.

Garnish with the remaining berries, the lemon zest, and a sprig of mint just before serving.

MAPLE DOUGHNUT HOLES

There is nothing like having a delicious, cakey doughnut that's freshly made and still piping hot. Even the best doughnut shops can't guarantee that! By making doughnut holes, you don't have to worry so much about shaping the dough, just rolling it with your hands—something most kids love to help out with.

This recipe calls for maple sugar, which is made from maple sap and can be found in many grocery stores or ordered online. It's a fun way to add even more maple flavor to your doughnuts, but if you can't find it, just substitute granulated sugar.

Makes 24 doughnut holes

1¾ cups all-purpose flour, plus more for dusting

½ cup white whole wheat flour

1 teaspoon baking powder

¼ teaspoon baking soda

¼ teaspoon ground nutmeg

¼ teaspoon kosher salt

½ cup plus 2 tablespoons maple sugar

1 large egg, at room temperature

½ cup buttermilk

¼ teaspoon grated lemon zest

1 tablespoon unsalted butter, melted

1 quart vegetable oil, for frying

¼ cup powdered sugar

1 tablespoon ground cinnamon

½ cup pure maple syrup

Line a large baking sheet with parchment paper and another with paper towels. Set a wire rack on top of the parchment-lined baking sheet.

In a large bowl, whisk together the flours, baking powder, baking soda, nutmeg, and salt.

In the bowl of a stand mixer fitted with the paddle attachment, combine ½ cup of the maple sugar, the egg, buttermilk, and lemon zest and beat on medium speed until creamy and caramel-colored. Add the flour mixture and then the butter, mixing until soft, sticky, and thick.

In a large, wide pot, heat the oil over medium heat to 350°F.

Turn the dough out onto a floured work surface and knead it a few times to bring it together and form a ball with a consistent texture. Using a well-floured rolling pin, roll the dough out to ⅓ inch thick. Use a floured 1½-inch round pastry cutter or a floured shot glass to cut as many disks as you can from the dough. Gather the remaining scraps into a ball, reroll, and, again, cut as many disks as you can. Repeat until all the dough has been used.

Gently roll each disk between the palms of your hands to form a ball.

Working in batches, use a slotted spoon or spider to carefully slide a few balls of dough into the hot oil. You don't want to crowd the pot or the temperature of the oil will drop and your doughnuts will not brown. The dough will sink at first and then quickly rise to the top. Fry the doughnut holes, using a slotted spoon or spider to turn them for even browning, until deep golden brown, 3 to 5 minutes. Transfer to the paper towel–lined baking sheet. Repeat until all the doughnut holes are fried, making sure the oil returns to 350°F before frying each batch.

In a small bowl, combine the powdered sugar, remaining 2 tablespoons maple sugar, and the cinnamon. Put the maple syrup in a separate small bowl.

While the doughnut holes are still warm, roll them in the maple syrup and transfer them to the wire rack on the baking sheet to drain. Use a fine-mesh sieve to dust a few spoonfuls of the powdered sugar mixture over the doughnut holes. Turn the doughnut holes over and repeat. Serve warm.

VANILLA BEAN BREAD PUDDING WITH BOURBON-CARAMEL SAUCE

I mean, sweet brioche soaked in vanilla custard and topped with bourbon-flavored caramel sauce? Not really sure there's more to say! This dessert could easily go from oven to table for a casual gathering, or slice it up and serve it in elegant glasses for a more polished effect.

Serves 4

FOR THE VANILLA BEAN BREAD PUDDING:

2 tablespoons unsalted butter, melted, plus more for greasing

2 cups whole milk

1 teaspoon vanilla bean paste (see Note, page 223)

⅓ cup granulated sugar

Pinch of kosher salt

4 large eggs, beaten

1 loaf brioche, cut into ½-inch cubes (5 to 6 cups)

FOR THE BOURBON-CARAMEL SAUCE:

1 cup granulated sugar

¼ teaspoon fresh lemon juice

4 tablespoons (½ stick) unsalted butter, cut into ½-inch cubes

1 cup heavy cream

2 tablespoons bourbon

½ teaspoon vanilla bean paste (see Note, page 223)

For the vanilla bean bread pudding: Preheat the oven to 350°F. Butter a 2-quart baking dish.

In a medium bowl, combine the milk, butter, vanilla bean paste, sugar, and salt. Whisk in the eggs and blend thoroughly.

Place the cubed brioche in the baking dish and pour the milk and egg mixture over it, stirring to coat all the bread. Let sit for at least 30 minutes.

Bake for 30 to 45 minutes, until the custard is set and the edges of the bread have browned.

For the bourbon-caramel sauce: In a medium saucepan, combine the sugar, lemon juice, and ¼ cup water. Bring to a boil over medium-high heat, stirring with a wooden spoon, and cook until the sugar becomes thick and dark amber in color, 10 to 12 minutes. Remove from the heat. The sugar should give off a burnt scent—sometimes the smell of burning in the kitchen is bad, but, in the case of sugar, it can actually be delicious. Using a wooden spoon, stir in the butter. Carefully add the cream, bourbon, and vanilla—the pot will vigorously bubble—and stir until fully blended.

Return the pan to the heat and cook until the sauce is thick enough to lightly coat the back of a spoon, another 10 minutes. Remove from the heat and let cool.

Drizzle the sauce liberally over the bread pudding and serve.

CHERRY GALETTE
WITH VANILLA WHIPPED CREAM

I'm a firm believer that everyone should have a go-to galette recipe. Because once you master the crust—which doesn't require any pastry skills whatsoever—there's nothing more to it than layering it up with your seasonal fruit of choice. If you can bake it in a pie, you can put it on a galette! It's rustic and free-form and couldn't look prettier on the table—especially dolloped with Vanilla Whipped Cream or ice cream and scattered with chopped nuts. Plus, it freezes especially well, so if you freeze a batch, you're never more than 20 minutes away from a gorgeous dessert.

Serves 4 to 6

FOR THE CRUST:

1 cup granulated sugar

1 cup nonhydrogenated vegetable shortening

¼ cup coconut oil, melted

⅛ teaspoon kosher salt

1 large egg

½ teaspoon vanilla bean paste (see Note, page 223)

2½ cups all-purpose flour, plus more for dusting

FOR THE FILLING:

2 tablespoons plus 1 teaspoon tapioca flour

2 tablespoons granulated sugar

⅛ teaspoon kosher salt

1½ pounds fresh red cherries, pitted

1 tablespoon fresh lemon juice

1 tablespoon brandy

½ teaspoon vanilla bean paste (see Note, page 223)

TO ASSEMBLE:

1 large egg, lightly beaten

1 tablespoon whole milk

2 tablespoons turbinado sugar

1 tablespoon sliced almonds, toasted (see Note, page 38)

Vanilla Whipped Cream (recipe follows), for serving

(Continued)

For the crust: In the bowl of a stand mixer fitted with the paddle attachment, beat together the granulated sugar, shortening, coconut oil, and salt on medium speed until light and fluffy, about 5 minutes. Stir in the egg and vanilla. Add the flour and mix on low until the dough comes together in a ball, about 2 minutes.

On a clean work surface, divide the dough in half and shape each piece into a disk. Wrap in plastic and refrigerate for 30 minutes or until ready to use. If you're only making 1 galette, store the second disk of dough in the freezer until you're in the mood to make another galette or pie.

For the filling: In a large bowl, whisk together the tapioca flour, granulated sugar, and salt. Add the cherries, lemon juice, brandy, and vanilla bean paste and toss gently to combine. Set aside.

To assemble: Preheat the oven to 400°F. Position a rack in the center of the oven.

Remove 1 disk of the dough from the refrigerator and leave at room temperature to soften, 10 to 15 minutes.

Roll out the dough between two sheets of lightly floured parchment paper into a 14-inch round. While still sandwiched between the sheets of parchment, transfer the dough to a large rimmed baking sheet and gently peel away the top sheet of parchment.

Spoon the filling into the center of the dough and spread it toward the edges, leaving a 2- to 2½-inch margin all the way around. Gently lift the edges of the parchment and use it to help you fold and crimp the exposed dough over the filling (the center will be open).

In a small bowl, whisk together the egg and milk and brush the mixture over the crust. Sprinkle with the turbinado sugar.

Bake for 40 to 50 minutes, rotating the baking sheet halfway through, until the crust is golden brown. Remove from the oven, sprinkle with the toasted almonds, and let cool slightly.

Serve with the Vanilla Whipped Cream.

VANILLA WHIPPED CREAM

Whipped cream is one of those things that is so easy to buy but *so* much better when homemade. There's nothing more to it than whipping together cream, sugar, and a hint of vanilla bean paste. Your guests will be impressed, I promise.

Makes about 3 cups

1½ cups heavy cream

2 tablespoons sugar

1 teaspoon vanilla bean paste (see Note, page 223)

In the bowl of a stand mixer fitted with the whisk attachment, whip the heavy cream until foamy. Add the sugar and vanilla and beat until the cream holds soft peaks. Do not overbeat, or the cream will become grainy. Serve immediately or cover and hold in the fridge overnight. You may need to rewhip the cream before serving, but just for a minute or two, until the cream regains its original volume.

SEA SALT–
CHOCOLATE CHIP COOKIES

Who doesn't love a chocolate chip cookie? They're such a nostalgic treat, bringing us back to childhood, whether your mom was baking them from scratch or throwing a sliced-up roll of Toll House in the oven. Served warm, they're pretty much the perfect dessert, and when stacked up in a mason jar with a cute little tag, they're just the thing for bake sales, picnics, hostess gifts, or goodie bags. You could also crumble them up and serve them on top of any sundae creation, or layer them with ice cream for ice cream sandwiches. I didn't want to mess with a good thing too much so I simply added a sprinkle of flaky sea salt, which doesn't taste salty so much as it brings out the sweetness of the chocolate.

Makes 12 cookies

1½ cups all-purpose flour

1 cup whole wheat flour

1 teaspoon baking powder

¼ teaspoon baking soda

1 cup (2 sticks) cold salted butter, cut into ½-inch cubes

1 cup firmly packed light brown sugar

½ cup granulated sugar

2 large eggs, beaten

2 teaspoons pure vanilla extract

2 cups semisweet chocolate chips

Flaky sea salt, for garnish

Place two silicone cookie molds with six 3.2-inch-wide, .7-inch-deep round cavities on a large baking sheet. (Alternatively, if you don't have molds, line a large baking sheet with parchment paper.)

In a medium bowl, combine the flours, baking powder, and baking soda. Set aside.

In the bowl of a stand mixer fitted with the paddle attachment, cream together the butter and sugars on medium speed until smooth. Add the eggs and vanilla and beat for 2 minutes. Gradually add the flour mixture and beat until combined. Use a wooden spoon or rubber spatula to gently fold in the chocolate chips. Divide the dough among the molds, filling each about three-quarters of the way. (If not using molds, divide the dough into 12 large balls and place each ball about 2 inches apart on the prepared baking sheet.) Sprinkle each cookie with a little sea salt. Cover and refrigerate overnight or freeze for 15 to 20 minutes.

Preheat the oven to 375°F.

Bake for 20 minutes, until the edges are golden brown. Let the cookies cool slightly before transferring them to a wire rack to cool completely. These will keep in an airtight container at room temperature for up to 1 week.

CHOCOLATE BARK, THREE WAYS

I almost didn't include this recipe because I was hesitant to give up one of my greatest secrets. People are always so impressed when I set out a batch of this bark as part of a dessert or snack spread or hand it out as a thanks-for-coming gift. Little do they know, I'm just melting down chocolate—dark, milk, or white—scattering it with any toppings that sound good—dried fruit, citrus zest, nuts, candies, cereal, edible flowers, just to name a few—and letting it set.

Serves 4

HAZELNUT, COFFEE, AND ORANGE ZEST BARK:

2 cups semisweet chocolate chips

¼ cup chopped hazelnuts

Grated zest of 1 large orange

½ teaspoon medium roast ground coffee

Flaky sea salt, for garnish

MAPLE BACON BARK:

2 cups milk chocolate chips

2 slices Maple-Fennel Bacon (page 19), finely chopped

Flaky sea salt, for garnish

LUCKY CHARMS BARK:

2 cups white chocolate

1½ cups Lucky Charms cereal

Flaky sea salt, for garnish

Line a large baking sheet with parchment paper.

Set a heatproof bowl over a pot of simmering water (the bottom of the bowl should not touch the water). Put the chocolate in the bowl and stir until melted and completely smooth. Depending on the bark you're making, mix in half the chopped hazelnuts, orange zest, and ground coffee; three-quarters of the Maple Bacon; or 1½ cups of the Lucky Charms. Immediately pour the mixture onto the prepared baking sheet and use a spatula to spread it into a thin layer. Sprinkle with the remaining toppings and flaky sea salt. Freeze for 15 minutes, or until firm.

Break up the bark into pieces and serve. The bark can also be stored in an airtight container at room temperature for up to 1 week or in the freezer for up to 1 month.

BLACKBERRY COBBLER

Blackberries are Harper's favorite, so when summer rolls around, I'm always looking for new ways to showcase them. Cobblers are the perfect way to serve just about any seasonal fruit, which gets tossed in a sugar-spice mix, then baked until warm and gooey under the crumble topping. Just like with my pizza dough, I like to throw in some whole wheat flour, which gives the cobbler topping a subtle nuttiness that's richer and more complex than if you use white flour alone. It's definitely a Penny-approved dessert!

Serves 6 to 8

FOR THE FILLING:

8 tablespoons (1 stick) unsalted butter, melted

4 cups fresh blackberries, washed and dried

⅔ cup granulated sugar

½ cup packed light brown sugar

1 teaspoon ground cinnamon

½ teaspoon ground nutmeg

½ teaspoon ground ginger

FOR THE CRUMBLE TOPPING:

⅔ cup whole milk

1 large egg

1 cup whole wheat flour

½ cup granulated sugar

2 teaspoons baking powder

¼ teaspoon kosher salt

Vanilla or Cinnamon Ice Cream (page 281) or store-bought, for serving

For the filling: Preheat the oven to 350°F. Coat a 9-by-13-inch baking dish with the melted butter.

In a medium bowl, combine the blackberries, sugars, cinnamon, nutmeg, and ginger. Spread the filling in the prepared baking dish.

For the crumble topping: In a small bowl, whisk together the milk and egg. Set aside.

In a large bowl, mix together the flour, granulated sugar, baking powder, and salt. Add the milk mixture and stir to combine. Pour the crumble topping over the filling; do not stir to combine.

Bake for 40 to 45 minutes, until the crumble topping has risen and is golden brown.

Serve warm or at room temperature with ice cream.

CHOCOLATE BISCOTTI

Somewhere along the line, "biscotti" started to be synonymous with "cardboard." True, these biscuits are supposed to have a drier, crispier texture than a typical cookie because they're double baked, but that shouldn't mean they have to be bland or boring. I give mine a lighter twist with almond flour and agave, but the deep chocolaty flavor they get from cocoa and espresso powders is anything but dainty. These are just as good a couple of days after you've made them as they are fresh out of the oven. In fact, I'd argue that I like them even more when they've had time to dry out a little because they're even better for dipping in coffee or tea. These are also the perfect treat for packing up in pretty bags or tins as gifts.

Makes 24 biscotti

2 cups all-purpose flour

1 cup almond flour

¼ cup unsweetened cocoa powder

2½ teaspoons baking powder

2 teaspoons instant espresso powder

¼ teaspoon kosher salt

1 cup sugar

8 tablespoons (1 stick) unsalted butter, at room temperature

3 large eggs plus 1 large egg white

1½ tablespoons agave nectar

1 tablespoon vanilla bean paste (see Note, page 223)

1 cup sliced almonds, toasted (see Note, page 38)

6 ounces semisweet chocolate, coarsely chopped

Preheat the oven to 350°F. Line a large baking sheet with parchment paper.

In a medium bowl, combine the flours, cocoa powder, baking powder, espresso powder, and salt. Set aside.

In the bowl of a stand mixer fitted with the paddle attachment, cream together the sugar and butter on medium speed for 2 minutes. One at a time, add the eggs and egg white and mix until completely incorporated. Mix in the agave and vanilla. Slowly add the flour mixture and mix just until incorporated. Turn off the machine and use a wooden spoon or rubber spatula to fold in the toasted almonds and chopped chocolate.

On the prepared baking sheet, divide the dough in half and shape it into two 8-by-13-inch rectangles. Bake for 35 minutes. Let the biscotti logs cool for 15 minutes. Transfer the logs to a cutting board and slice them into ½-inch-thick pieces. Return the biscotti cut-side down to the prepared baking sheet and bake for 18 to 20 minutes more, until golden. Transfer to a wire rack to cool before serving. These will keep in an airtight container at room temperature for up to 1 week.

STRAWBERRY SHORTCAKE ICE CREAM SANDWICHES

Homemade strawberry ice cream sandwiched between two buttery shortcake-style cookies and sprinkled with freeze-dried berries says "summer" like nobody's business, all in one cute little handheld treat.

Makes 6 ice cream sandwiches

FOR THE STRAWBERRY ICE CREAM:

1 batch Strawberries & Cream Ice Cream (page 281), or 2 quarts store-bought, softened

FOR THE SHORTBREAD COOKIES:

1½ cups (3 sticks) cold unsalted butter, cut into ½-inch cubes

¾ cup sugar

1 tablespoon pure vanilla extract

3 cups all-purpose flour

½ teaspoon kosher salt

TO ASSEMBLE:

½ cup crushed freeze-dried strawberries

For the strawberry ice cream: Line a 9½-by-13-inch rimmed baking sheet with parchment paper and evenly spread the ice cream over the baking sheet. Freeze until firm, 6 to 8 hours.

For the shortbread cookies: In the bowl of a stand mixer fitted with the paddle attachment, cream the butter and sugar on medium speed until smooth. Add the vanilla. Gradually add the flour and salt and mix until just combined. Turn out the dough onto a clean work surface and shape it into a disk. Wrap in plastic and refrigerate for 30 minutes.

Preheat the oven to 350°F.

Place the dough on a sheet of parchment paper that's roughly the size of a large baking sheet. Roll out the dough to ¼ inch thick, making sure it's no larger than the parchment. Carefully transfer the parchment with the dough onto a baking sheet and bake for 18 to 20 minutes, until golden. Let the baked dough cool for 10 to 12 minutes, then use a 3-inch biscuit cutter to cut out 12 rounds. It's important to cut the cookies while they are still slightly warm or they will not cut as cleanly. Discard the scraps (and by that I mean eat them or save them for your next piecrust) and let the cookies cool completely.

To assemble: Remove the ice cream from the freezer and use the 3-inch biscuit cutter to make 6 rounds, saving any scraps in an airtight container to crumble over ice cream later. Place each ice cream disk on top of a shortbread cookie and top with a second cookie to create a sandwich.

Scatter the crushed freeze-dried strawberries on a plate. Roll the edges of each sandwich in the fruit. Serve immediately or store in an airtight container in the freezer for up to 2 weeks.

HOT CHOCOLATE AFFOGATO WITH CINNAMON ICE CREAM

This Italian version of a root beer float is usually made with coffee or espresso, but I've made it kid-friendly by switching to hot chocolate instead. Served in matching mugs with cinnamon stick stirrers, it's the ultimate cozy delight that's begging for matching flannel PJs and a fire in the fireplace.

Serves 2

4 cups whole milk

½ cup unsweetened cocoa powder

½ cup granulated sugar

¼ teaspoon kosher salt

1 teaspoon pure vanilla extract

4 scoops Cinnamon Ice Cream (page 281) or store-bought

2 cinnamon sticks, for serving

In a medium saucepan, combine the milk, cocoa powder, sugar, salt, and vanilla. Heat over medium heat, stirring, until the sugar has dissolved and no lumps remain. Bring the mixture to a simmer, stirring continuously, and cook until hot, about 4 minutes. Remove from the heat and set aside.

Place 2 small scoops of the Cinnamon Ice Cream in each mug, then pour in the hot chocolate. Garnish with a cinnamon stick stirrer and serve.

KEY LIME BARS

My dad loves key lime anything—pie, bars, cheesecake. I've come to love its bright, tart flavor, especially as a refreshing counterpart to heavier, richer desserts. While key limes are what give these bars their signature flavor, you could use regular limes and still end up with a perfectly puckery dessert.

Makes 8 bars

FOR THE CRUST:

1 cup all-purpose flour

¼ cup powdered sugar, plus more for dusting

Pinch of kosher salt

8 tablespoons (1 stick) cold unsalted butter, cut into ½-inch cubes

FOR THE TOPPING:

3 large eggs, at room temperature

1½ cups granulated sugar

Pinch of kosher salt

¼ cup all-purpose flour

1 teaspoon grated key lime zest

½ cup key lime juice (from about ¾ pound key limes)

For the crust: Preheat the oven to 350°F. Line an 8-inch square baking pan with parchment paper.

In a large bowl, whisk together the flour, powdered sugar, and salt. Use your hands or a pastry blender to work the butter into the flour mixture until pea-size pieces form. Press the crust evenly into the prepared pan and bake for 20 minutes, or until the crust is golden brown. Set aside and reduce the oven temperature to 325°F.

For the topping: In a large bowl, whisk together the eggs, sugar, and salt until light yellow and creamy. Whisk in the flour until well incorporated. Add the key lime zest and juice and whisk until smooth.

Pour the key lime topping over the crust and return the pan to the oven. Bake for 30 minutes, or until the topping is set but still jiggles when you lightly move the pan.

Dust with powdered sugar while still hot, then let cool completely before cutting into 8 bars.

COCONUT-KAHLÚA
RICE PUDDING

Rice pudding has always been one of Mom's favorite desserts. Here I've just dressed it up with coconut flakes and coconut milk, plus a dash of Kahlúa. It's just as good served hot off the stovetop as it is chilled.

Serves 2 or 3

1 cup Arborio rice

1 cup unsweetened shredded coconut

1 (13.5-ounce) can unsweetened full-fat coconut milk

2 tablespoons Kahlúa or other coffee liqueur

1 teaspoon vanilla bean paste (see Note, page 223)

1 teaspoon coconut extract

½ cup sweetened condensed milk

Bring 4 cups water to a boil in a medium pot over medium heat. Add the rice and cook until it has softened but still has bite, about 15 minutes.

While the rice is cooking, toast half the shredded coconut in a small sauté pan, stirring often, until golden brown, 3 to 4 minutes. Set aside.

Drain the rice and return it to the pot. Add the coconut milk, ½ cup of the untoasted shredded coconut, the Kahlúa, vanilla, and coconut extract. Bring to a simmer over low heat and cook, stirring continuously, for 15 to 20 minutes, until the rice is tender and the pudding is thick. Stir in the condensed milk.

Ladle the pudding into serving dishes and top with the toasted coconut. Or let the pudding cool to room temperature, then chill in the refrigerator until ready to serve.

NAKED CARROT CAKE

I was so excited when the newest trend in pastries was the "naked" cake, or tiered cakes that were barely smeared with the filling instead of being spackled with buttercream. It's amazing how elegant something so unfussy can look, and I can't say that I miss all that heavy icing. I decided to give my tried-and-true carrot cake recipe a dressed-down makeover, and the result is the perfect ratio between moist cake and just-sweet-enough orange-scented cream cheese frosting. You could absolutely serve this during the week, but it's got "special occasion" written all over it.

Makes one 9-inch triple-layer cake

FOR THE CAKE:

Nonstick cooking spray

3 cups all-purpose flour

1 tablespoon baking powder

2 teaspoons baking soda

2 teaspoons ground cinnamon

1 teaspoon ground ginger

2½ cups packed light brown sugar

1½ cups vegetable oil

6 large eggs, at room temperature

2 teaspoons vanilla bean paste
(see Note, page 223)

4 cups grated carrot
(about 1½ pounds carrots)

1 (20-ounce) can crushed pineapple,
drained (about 1½ cups)

1 cup chopped pecans

FOR THE FROSTING:

4 (8-ounce) packages cream
cheese, at room temperature

1 cup (2 sticks) unsalted butter

4 cups powdered sugar

2 tablespoons orange extract

Grated zest of 2 oranges, plus more
for garnish

1 medium carrot, spiralized,
for garnish

(Continued)

For the cake: Preheat the oven to 350°F. Line three 9-inch round baking pans with parchment paper cut to fit and spray the sides with cooking spray.

In a medium bowl, whisk together the flour, baking powder, baking soda, cinnamon, and ginger.

In a large bowl using a handheld mixer or in the bowl of a stand mixer fitted with the paddle attachment, beat together the brown sugar and oil on low speed until fully combined, 2 to 3 minutes. Add the eggs one at a time, then add the vanilla. Scrape down the sides to ensure that everything is incorporated. Gently stir in the flour mixture by hand until just combined. Fold in the carrots, pineapple, and pecans. Do not overmix.

Evenly distribute the batter among the prepared pans and bake for 40 to 50 minutes, until the cakes are fully set and a toothpick inserted into the middle comes out clean. Cool completely in the pans, about 1 hour.

For the frosting: In a large bowl using a handheld mixer or in the bowl of a stand mixer fitted with the paddle attachment, beat the cream cheese, butter, powdered sugar, orange extract, and orange zest until smooth and fluffy, 2 to 3 minutes.

To assemble: Remove the cake layers from the pans when completely cool. Place 1 layer on a cake plate and, using an offset spatula, spread a quarter of the frosting over top of the layer, taking care to spread it all the way to the edges. It's okay if some of the frosting goes onto the sides (I like it better when it's not perfect). Stack the second layer on top of the first, add another quarter of the frosting, and repeat with the remaining layers. Use the remaining frosting to lightly coat the sides of the cake so you can still can see the cake through the frosting.

Scatter the orange zest over the top and garnish with spiralized carrot.

Candied Ginger Apple Pie (page 272)

CANDIED GINGER APPLE PIE

I can't make a pie without feeling like I'm ten years old and standing next to my grandmother in the kitchen. Pies are just special that way. Apple pie has such a feel-good, All-American vibe, especially the way it makes the house smell when it's in the oven. My version stays pretty true to the classic but with the addition of ginger for the tiniest hint of fresh zing. It doesn't overpower the apples, just adds a little warmth.

Makes one 9-inch pie

FOR THE CRUST:

2½ cups all-purpose flour

1 tablespoon sugar

¾ teaspoon kosher salt

1 cup (2 sticks) cold unsalted butter, cut into ½-inch cubes

¼ cup ice water, plus more as needed

FOR THE FILLING:

3 Granny Smith apples, peeled, cored, and thinly sliced

3 McIntosh apples, peeled, cored, and thinly sliced

⅔ cup sugar

3 tablespoons finely chopped crystallized ginger

2 tablespoons cornstarch

1 tablespoon fresh lemon juice

1 teaspoon ground cinnamon

1 teaspoon vanilla bean paste (see Note, page 223)

Pinch of kosher salt

TO ASSEMBLE:

1 large egg

Vanilla Ice Cream (page 281) or store-bought, for serving

Preheat the oven to 425°F. Place a 9-inch pie dish on a baking sheet.

For the crust: In a food processor, combine the flour, sugar, and salt. Pulse a few times to combine. Add the butter and pulse a few more times until the mixture resembles fine gravel. Add the ice water, a few tablespoons at a time, until the dough comes together and forms a ball. Remove the dough from the food processor and divide it into 2 disks. Wrap each disk in plastic and refrigerate for at least 30 minutes.

For the filling: In a large bowl, combine the sliced apples, sugar, ginger, cornstarch, lemon juice, cinnamon, vanilla, and salt.

To assemble: Remove 1 disk of the dough from the refrigerator and, if necessary, let it sit at room temperature for about 10 minutes to soften. On a floured surface, roll out the disk to form a ⅛-inch-thick, 12-inch-wide round. Transfer to the pie dish and gently press the dough into the pan, eliminating any air pockets. Trim the overhanging dough to ½ inch. Spoon the filling over the dough.

To make the top of the pie, roll out the second dough disk to the same width and thickness as the first. From here, you can show off your pastry skills by making a lattice top (check out YouTube for some gorgeous variations—which is what I did to create this one here!), or you can simply lay the rolled dough over the top of the pie. Either way, fold the top crust edges over the overhang of the bottom crust to create a seal, trimming as needed. Crimp the edges by pinching the dough between your thumb and forefinger. Use a sharp knife to cut six vents into the top crust if you choose to use a simple rolled-out top crust.

In a small bowl, beat the egg with 1 tablespoon water. Using a pastry brush, lightly brush the crust with the egg wash.

Using aluminum foil, make a "collar" just around the edges of the pie crust to prevent them from browning too quickly. Bake for 15 minutes, then reduce the oven temperature to 350°F. Bake until the crust is golden brown and the filling is bubbling, about 1 hour, removing the foil collar for the last 10 to 15 minutes.

Transfer the pie to a wire rack and cool completely. Serve with a scoop of vanilla ice cream.

GRILLED PEACHES WITH HOMEMADE LEMON RICOTTA & HONEY

Okay, I know I'm the first person to go messing around with the classic, traditional, and otherwise perfect. But there are some things that are just meant to be simple. Grilled fruit is one of them. This amazing thing happens when you char it lightly—the sugars caramelize, giving the fruit deeper, pie filling–like flavor, with just a hint of smokiness. And don't reserve this special treatment for peaches; it's just as delicious with any other stone fruit like plums or nectarines, tropical varieties like mango or pineapple, or even cherries or bananas.

This dessert doesn't need anything else, except maybe a scoop of cool homemade ricotta whipped with yogurt and brightened with lemon. It's almost hard to believe that three simple ingredients and minimal hands-on prep can yield the creamiest, most delicious cheese. The extra-mile element really elevates this otherwise crazy-simple dessert. You can store leftovers in the fridge for dolloping on top of just about anything—pizza, pasta, toast, granola, or fresh fruit.

Serves 4

2 cups Homemade Ricotta (recipe follows) or store-bought

1 cup plain whole-milk Greek yogurt

2 tablespoons fresh lemon juice (from 1 lemon)

4 large yellow peaches, halved and pitted

2 tablespoons honey (preferably wildflower)

Grated zest of 1 lemon, for garnish

2 tablespoons chopped pistachios, for garnish

Preheat a grill pan over medium-high heat or heat an outdoor grill to medium high.

In the bowl of a stand mixer fitted with the paddle attachment, combine the ricotta, yogurt, and lemon juice. Whip on medium speed until combined and fluffy, about 1 minute. Set aside.

Place the peach halves on the grill pan or grill. Cook for 4 minutes per side, creating nice grill marks.

Transfer the peaches to a plate. Serve each with the lemon ricotta, a drizzle of honey, a dash of lemon zest, and a sprinkling of pistachios.

(Continued)

HOMEMADE RICOTTA

Makes 2 cups

8 cups whole milk

⅓ cup fresh lemon juice
(from about 3 lemons),
plus more as needed

1 teaspoon kosher salt

In a medium pot, gently heat the milk over medium heat to 200°F. When the milk is foamy and steaming but not yet boiling, remove it from the heat. Gently stir in the lemon juice and salt and let sit until the milk separates into curds, about 10 minutes. If there is still a lot of unseparated milk after 10 minutes, add a bit more lemon juice and let it sit for another few minutes.

Line a strainer with four or five layers of cheesecloth and place it over a large bowl. Gently pour the cheese curds and liquid (whey) into the strainer to drain. The longer you let your ricotta drain, the thicker it will be. For a looser ricotta, drain for no more than 5 minutes. For drier ricotta, drain for 15 minutes or longer.

Enjoy fresh, or refrigerate in an airtight container for up to 1 week. And don't throw away your whey! You can use it in doughs; add it to pasta dishes, soups, and sauces for a tangy flavor; or even water your plants with it!

MASCARPONE, HONEY & STRAWBERRY PIZZA

Pizza night is a regular in our dinner rotation, and I always like to get the kids involved, especially when it comes to picking out their favorite toppings (a surefire way to get them to eat the finished product!). One time, Harper grabbed creamy cheese and strawberries out of the fridge, and that's how dessert pizza was born. I use the same dough recipe as the savory versions but sweeten it up just a touch with sugar and cinnamon.

Serves 2 to 4

½ cup mascarpone, at room temperature

½ cup plain whole-milk Greek yogurt

3 tablespoons honey, plus more for serving

1 cooked From-Scratch Grilled Pizza Crust (page 164)

½ cup fresh strawberries, washed, dried, stemmed, and sliced

Grated zest of ½ lemon

Preheat the oven to 400°F.

In a small bowl, combine the mascarpone, yogurt, and honey. Spread the mixture over the crust and scatter the strawberries evenly over the top.

Bake for 10 to 15 minutes, until the strawberries have softened and released some of their juices. Remove from the oven, drizzle with honey, and garnish with lemon zest.

ICE CREAMS

Making ice cream from scratch is one of my favorite things to do in the summer. We do it at least once a week, and I especially love getting the kids involved, whether they're throwing in bits of fruit, nuts, or candy or keeping an eye on the ice cream machine as it churns. There are a lot of different ways to make an ice cream base: with eggs, with milk and cream, without any dairy at all. Here I've given my favorite variations for all three. They're all incredibly easy to make, especially if you have an ice cream maker. You don't need a big mac daddy one—just something basic will do.

I've also included my favorite sundae topper—chocolate shell. It's has the same fun, fudgy-yet-crunchy consistency as store-bought Magic Shell, except it uses only two ingredients (chocolate and coconut oil) and is impossibly easy to make yourself.

Coconut Ice Cream (p. 282)

CHOOSE YOUR FLAVOR

Makes 1 quart

FOR THE PLAIN BASE:

2 large eggs

2 cups heavy cream

1 cup whole milk

1 cup sugar

FLAVOR ADD-IN EXAMPLES:

Vanilla:
1 teaspoon pure vanilla extract

Cinnamon:
1 teaspoon pure vanilla extract and
2 teaspoons ground cinnamon

In a medium heatproof glass bowl, whisk together the eggs. Gradually whisk in the cream and milk until incorporated. Add the sugar a little at a time and whisk until completely dissolved.

Set the bowl over a pot of simmering water over low heat (the bottom of the bowl should not touch the water). Heat the egg mixture, stirring occasionally, until it coats the back of a spoon, about 40 minutes. Remove the bowl from the heat and stir in the vanilla or cinnamon flavor additions. Pour the mixture into an ice cream maker and freeze according to the manufacturer's instructions. Transfer to an airtight container and store in the freezer.

STRAWBERRIES & CREAM

Makes 1½ quarts

1 pound fresh strawberries, washed, dried, stemmed, and thinly sliced

1½ cups sugar

1½ cups whole milk

1½ cups skim milk

2 cups heavy cream

Place the strawberries and ½ cup of the sugar in a shallow bowl and stir to coat the strawberries. Cover and set aside for 6 to 8 hours; the strawberries will begin to release liquid.

In a blender, combine the strawberries and their liquid, the milks, heavy cream, and remaining 1 cup sugar and blend until smooth. Pour the mixture into an ice cream maker and freeze according to the manufacturer's instructions. Transfer to an airtight container and store in the freezer.

COCONUT ICE CREAM

Makes 1 quart

2 (14-ounce) cans unsweetened
full-fat coconut milk

1 tablespoon agave nectar

2 teaspoons vanilla bean paste
(see Note, page 223)

½ cup sugar

In a medium bowl, whisk together the coconut milk, agave, and vanilla. While whisking, add the sugar a little at a time until completely incorporated. Pour the mixture into an ice cream maker and freeze according to the manufacturer's instructions. Take a taste, trying not to eat it all, then transfer to an airtight container and store in the freezer until ready to serve.

CHOCOLATE SHELL

Makes 1 cup

1 cup semisweet chocolate chips

2 tablespoons coconut oil

In a heatproof glass bowl set over a pot of simmering water (the bottom of the bowl should not touch the water), melt the chocolate chips and coconut oil, stirring often, until smooth and silky.

To serve, generously drizzle the chocolate over a bowl of ice cream and let it cool to set. You'll know it's ready when it turns from shiny to matte. Top with your favorite sundae fixins like toasted shredded coconut or sprinkles, then break open the shell with a big ol' spoon and enjoy.

GIRL SCOUT COOKIE ICEBOX CAKE

Icebox cake is, in its simplest form, chocolate wafers layered high with whipped cream then frozen until you can slice it just like cake. It's adorably old-school and also the quintessential summer dessert (no hot oven required), so I was inspired to give it an updated twist. Harper just joined the Girl Scouts, which means there's no shortage of cookies in our house. And the hands-down favorite that gets even better chilled in the freezer? Thin Mints! They were the obvious choice for this new-and-improved dessert.

Makes one 9-inch cake

FOR THE WHIPPED CREAM:

6 cups heavy cream, chilled

6 tablespoons granulated sugar

2 tablespoons vanilla bean paste (see Note, page 223)

TO ASSEMBLE:

4 (9-ounce) boxes Thin Mints

Dark chocolate shavings

1 sprig fresh mint

For the whipped cream: In the bowl of a stand mixer fitted with the whisk attachment or in a large bowl with a whisk or handheld mixer, whip the cream until slightly foamy. Add the sugar and vanilla and beat on high speed until the cream holds soft peaks.

To assemble: On a round 12-inch serving platter, arrange 1 sleeve of cookies (approximately 16 cookies) in a circle to form the cake's base layer. Use an offset spatula to spread ¾ cup of the whipped cream evenly over the cookie layer. Repeat both steps until you have added 8 layers of cookies and 8 layers of whipped cream. Place the cake in the freezer for at least 4 hours.

Garnish with dark chocolate shavings and a sprig of fresh mint and serve.

AVOCADO BROWNIES

One of my favorite new baking trends—aside from naked cakes (see page 267)—is using avocados in place of some of the butter in a recipe. Since we're big avocado fans in this house—and I love any excuse to make more brownies—I figured out how to turn my fudgy, cakey go-to recipe into a slightly healthier one. It turns out that you don't taste the avocado whatsoever, but you get all its rich creaminess thanks to the natural oils.

Makes 9 brownies

Nonstick cooking spray

1⅓ cups all-purpose flour

¾ cup unsweetened cocoa powder

½ teaspoon kosher salt

¼ teaspoon baking powder

1½ cups granulated sugar

4 large eggs, at room temperature

2 teaspoons pure vanilla extract

½ teaspoon espresso powder

8 tablespoons (1 stick) unsalted butter

1½ cups packed light brown sugar

½ very ripe avocado, pureed in a blender until smooth

4 ounces semisweet chocolate chips, melted

1 ounce unsweetened chocolate, melted

Preheat the oven to 350°F. Line an 8-inch square baking pan with parchment paper and spray it with cooking spray.

In a large bowl, whisk together the flour, cocoa powder, salt, and baking powder. Set aside.

In a medium bowl, whisk ½ cup of the granulated sugar and the eggs until the sugar has dissolved. Stir in the pure vanilla and espresso powder. Set aside.

In the bowl of a stand mixer fitted with the paddle attachment, cream together the butter, remaining 1 cup granulated sugar, and the brown sugar on medium speed until combined. Add the avocado puree and mix until well combined. Add the egg mixture in three additions, beating well after each. Reduce the speed to low and gently mix in the melted chocolate. Add the flour mixture in batches until blended, taking care to scrape down the sides and bottom of the bowl as needed. The batter will be thick.

Pour the batter into the prepared baking pan and bake for 50 to 60 minutes, until a toothpick inserted into the center comes out clean. Let the brownies cool before cutting and serving.

PICTURE-PERFECT
PARTIES

I n my book, a gathering doesn't need to include much more than good food and good company to be considered a party. But for the moments when you want to put together a nice little something for friends and family, I've included some of my favorite celebration concepts, from newspaper-as-tablecloth casual to all-dressed-up chic. You'll find suggested menus (all assembled from the recipes in this book), décor tips, and ideas for how to mark the occasion in a thoughtful, unique way, whether you're adding impressive homemade elements (bottled from-scratch sodas!) or sending guests home with favors (granola and jam for the next morning!). I've also thrown in my tried-and-true planning checklist, which is a must if you're going to entertain without losing your cool. All of these tools will help you organize parties that feel warm, special, and, most important, *easy*. The best party is the one that you get to enjoy yourself. Have fun!

PULL UP A CHAIR PLANNING CHECKLIST

I am notorious for my lists—everyone in my house knows that if there's company coming over, then there's a list of things that need to get done before the first guest rings the doorbell. Whether it's grocery shopping, setting out the food, or even getting the kids (and myself!) dressed, if it needs doing, it's on the list. Then I stick it in my kitchen, check things off as they get done, and feel much more cool and collected come party time—no matter how many little bumps in the road there might be.

I've always been super-organized (okay, totally type A), ever since I was a little girl, packing my suitcase weeks in advance before I'd leave for a trip. Luckily, that kind of planning comes in handy when it's time to get prepped for a gathering. It not only ensures that the event itself will run more smoothly, but also makes having people over so much less stressful. This way you can give yourself a few days to get everything in order, won't forget a single detail, and can actually enjoy yourself on the day of.

This is what my list looks like for most of my parties. Of course, the bigger a "to-do" your event is, the more detailed the list might be. If you're arranging outside help like hiring a rental company, florist, or entertainment, then you can build that in. More casual gatherings will be more pared down. The key is spreading everything out so it never feels like you're on party-planning overload. Remember: It should be fun!

7 DAYS BEFORE THE PARTY:

Write your menu (don't forget to ask guests if there are any food restrictions!).

Brainstorm themes for the occasion and jot down décor ideas (I love Pinterest for this).

5 DAYS BEFORE THE PARTY:

Shop for nonperishables and alcohol.

Hit up a party goods store for theme-specific decorations or any other tablescape details.

Clean and iron your linens or have them pressed.

3 DAYS BEFORE THE PARTY:

Shop for perishables.

Start light prep, i.e., wash and chop veggies, make marinades or dressings, churn and freeze ice cream.

Round up your serving ware, dinnerware, glassware, and flatware, and figure out which platters or serving bowls you'll use for each dish. Give everything a good wipe down if it's been a while since it was last used.

DAY BEFORE THE PARTY:

Cook any dishes that can be held in the fridge and reheated before serving.

Plate any menu components that will be served chilled or at room temperature, i.e., put spreads in pretty bowls or arrange crudités on a platter. Cover with plastic wrap and store in the fridge so all you have to do is unwrap and serve.

Set the table.

Send a "Can't wait to see you!" message (and gentle reminder) to guests.

Buy flowers for floral arrangements.

PARTY DAY:

Stock up on ice.

Finish cooking.

Arrange floral and décor.

Snap a few pics of your hard work.

Get everyone dressed (including you!).

Party time!

BREAKFAST IN BED

MENU

Green Smoothies (page 4)

Cherry & Maple Granola (page 34)

Yogurt Pancakes with Whipped Maple Butter (page 45)

French press coffee, tea, and juice

I have a feeling that I'm not the only one who daydreams of spending all morning in bed, lounging in my cutest, comfiest PJs and nibbling on homemade granola, a stack of piping hot pancakes, a fresh green smoothie, and all the coffee I can drink. It's absolutely worth it to get up a little bit early to make this spread for you and your honey, especially on Valentine's Day, Mother's or Father's Day, an anniversary—or any other weekend when your kids are with the grandparents! You could also throw a breakfast-in-bed-style party for friends, sans bed. Have everyone come over in their most stylish sleepwear and enjoy the same spread. Whether it's for a party of two or twenty, almost all these dishes can be prepped ahead, which means you can sleep in.

The Vibe: Lazy Day Made Lovely

The Food: Almost everything on this menu can be made or prepped in advance. The granola will stay fresh in an airtight container for at least a week, so all you need to do in the morning is pour servings into individual bowls or layer it with yogurt to make parfaits. The pancake batter can sit in the fridge overnight, along with the maple butter; you can portion out the smoothie ingredients; and you can have lots of sliced fresh fruit or bowls of berries ready to go. Serve with plenty of fresh juice and coffee and a selection of teas. If it's just two of you, a really nice touch is single-serving French presses.

The Décor: Arrange trays with your prettiest bowls, plates, glasses, and teacups—break out the china, if you have it! Add a spray of fresh-cut flowers and whatever other touches say breakfast to you, like a rolled-up newspaper, a crossword puzzle, or the Sunday comics.

The Special Touch: If you're having guests, send them home with their own parcels of granola and maybe a container of Homemade Jam (page 9).

LADIES WHO LUNCH

MENU

Creamy Sweet Corn Soup (page 53)

Lobster BLT Lettuce Wraps (page 77)

Cherry Galette with Vanilla Whipped Cream (page 245)

Hibiscus Spritzers (page 212)

Even though I'm usually all about the down-home spirit, I also really love the chance to take things in a more elegant direction. Every once in a while I'll host an afternoon luncheon for the girls so we can relax and catch up, and I use it as an excuse to pull out my finest—both from my kitchen and my closet. The food itself doesn't necessarily have to be fancy; it's all in the details. A simple bowl of soup gets that much lovelier in a pretty bowl with delicate garnishes. A Lobster BLT is downright refined served over a bed of greens. No matter what you decide to have on the menu, it's all about presentation. Take a moment to think about how you can make the food look that much more inviting or your guests feel that much more welcome.

The Vibe: Garden Party Glamour

The Food: This menu takes the usual luncheon suspects—soup, salad, and dessert—and gives them a more polished presentation.

The Décor: Capture the garden party feel with pretty pastels and tons of flowers. For gorgeous floral arrangements on a budget, go to the grocery store and see what you can find in the same color family. Bundle them together in a big, beautiful bouquet and put them in your most special vase. Even a tall glass jar, milk jug, or pitcher will do the trick. This is also the time to pull out all your favorite linens and place settings. If you don't have things like chargers, runners, or serving pieces that you love, see what you can find at a local flea market or discount store. If your plates and glasses are simple, you can get away with mixing patterns and shapes for your other pieces.

The Special Touch: Make a signature cocktail like Hibiscus Spritzers, hibiscus tea–infused prosecco with a touch of mint simple syrup. It's a light, refreshing drink that won't leave you or your guests out of commission for the rest of the day. Be sure to toast to one another and thank everyone for their friendship and support.

MEXI-CALI FIESTA

MENU

Cauliflower "Chorizo" Tacos with Cuban-Style Black Beans (page 138)

Homemade Tortilla Chips (page 201), Tropical Salsa (page 199),
and Classic or Mango Guacamole (page 200 or 28)

Watermelon-Mint Margaritas (page 217)

There's no wrong way to fiesta—just celebrate the people you love with great food and fun music. It's also a great excuse to pull out all your favorite Mexican (or Latin American, in the case of my all-time favorite Cuban-Style Black Beans) dishes, whether it's for a summer backyard gathering or a dose of sunshine in the middle of winter.

The Vibe: Southern California Meets South of the Border

The Food: Anything you can pile up on tortillas—corn, flour, or both—plus plenty of dips. Serve with Mexican beer and watermelon and mint-infused margaritas, plus Topo Chico sparkling water and Jarritos Mexican sodas.

The Décor: Add a little flair with serapes as tablecloths, or just keep it simple and go for a lot of bold color with your linens and napkins. Earthenware bowls and plates add festive warmth, as do napkin-lined plates piled high with still-warm tortillas and brown paper bags folded over at the top and heaped with homemade chips. Or go the quirky route by using empty Mexican canned goods for utensil holders or vases. El Pato green enchilada sauce has a particularly pretty label, and you can order it by the case online.

The Special Touch: Offer guests fresh-flower headpieces or set up a station where they get to assemble their own. Then send everyone home with a bottle of your favorite hot sauce with a "thanks for coming!" note attached.

BRADY BOIL

MENU

Lobster Boil (page 129)

Pimento Cheese (page 174)

Key Lime Bars (page 264)

Peach-Jalapeño Texas Tea (page 218)

If there's one thing that makes me want to up and move to the East Coast, it's a classic New England–style lobster boil. You probably know what I'm talking about—an enormous pot of corn, sausages, potatoes, clams, and, of course, lobster, all simmered in an aromatic lager broth, then sloshed over a newspaper-covered table for everyone to dig into with their hands. Since this is also one of Brady's favorite summer rituals, I decided to plan a party around some of his other favorite things, including Pimento Cheese Dip and wouldn't-be-a-party-without-it tequila-spiked Texas tea.

The Vibe: The Northeast Heads South

The Food: This is the definition of a one-pot meal, so you don't need to serve much more than something for guests to snack on while the lobsters are cooking. Pimento Cheese Dip brings in some decadent Southern flair, while Key Lime Bars are a play on the classic lemon version that you'll find at pretty much every picnic below the Mason-Dixon Line.

The Décor: The look of this dinner is all about bringing the Maine beach to you. You could just drape your table in newspaper and scatter a few mallets on top and be good to go. Or you can add sweet touches like sand- or pebble-filled mason jars with tea lights set on top or silverware bundled in twine. I also like to highlight the colors of the meal—the vibrant red of the lobster and yellow of the corn. You can tie these elements in with your napkins or dishware—lobster motif (including bibs!) encouraged but optional.

The Special Touch: When I'm bringing the bar outside for a casual gathering, I like to fill big galvanized tubs with ice, then load them up with beers, wine, and sparkling water.

PIZZA PARTY

MENU

Nectarine Caprese Salad (page 67)

Arugula, Grape & Ricotta Pizza (page 162)

Spicy Sausage, Garlic Kale & Goat Cheese Pizza (page 158)

Broccoli Rabe, Prosciutto & Burrata Pizza (page 161)

Blood Orange–Rosé Sangria (page 219)

There's a reason why pizza night is a regular occurrence in our house. It's super quick to pull together; there's enough variety to make everyone happy. The same goes for having people over. This is such an easy concept to suit both small and large crowds—plus, you can have fun with the theme (Tony's Pizzeria or Tuscany at Dusk?), and the flavor combinations that you can throw together on my grilled pizza crust are endless. It's an amazing day when you have a house full of company and pizza!

The Vibe: Mangia, Mangia, Mangia!

The Food: Aim for three or four different kinds, and a nice, light salad, like a Nectarine Caprese, my unique twist on the light, classic Italian dish. Set out a hunk of fresh Parm and a grater so people can sprinkle their own, then add a big pitcher of Blood Orange–Rosé Sangria—the perfect refreshing accompaniment to the pizza, and a few different kinds of beer or bottles of Italian wine.

The Décor: Are you going classic pizzeria with red-and-white checkered tablecloths, Parmesan and crushed red pepper shakers, and ample bottles of house red; taking things to the Italian countryside with earth-toned linens and rustic wicker chargers; or inviting everyone to crowd around a butcher paper–lined kitchen island or dining room table to eat standing up? Think about scattering the table with big wooden boards to rest the pizzas on—plus, they really complement the au naturale look of the slightly charred, perfectly imperfect pizzas.

The Special Touch: I like to label each of the pizzas. If I'm using butcher paper on the table, I'll write the name of the pies right on there. Or if I'm going a little more formal, I'll set out a chalk-board with the menu. Then let your kids help decorate!

ALL-DRESSED-UP COCKTAIL HOUR

MENU

Honey-Ginger Chicken Wings (page 194)

Eggplant Crisps with Rosemary-Infused Honey Drizzle (page 196)

Whiskey-Glazed Spiced Nuts (page 170)

Cheese Biscuit Crackers (page 171)

Peanut Butter & Chocolate Bites (page 231)

Blackberry-Basil Smash (page 208)

I don't know about you, but there are some days when I can't remember the last time I wasn't wearing some variation of workout clothes. That's the mom life! Though, to be honest, I sure did love me some sweatpants before I had kids, too . . . either way, when I start looking at all the pretty dress-up clothes in my closet, I know it's time to host an all-dolled-up—but simple-to-throw-together—cocktail party. I invite a small group of friends—enough to fill a room, but not so many that we can't all sit and chat—and relish the opportunity to catch up with grown-up conversation. No sitter required!

The Vibe: Elegant but Easy

The Food: It should feel like you're nibbling on hors d'oeuvres from passed trays—without any leg-work. Perfect party treats like these finger foods take no time to make and can be prepped ahead. Then round out the selection with store-bought items like cheeses, charcuterie, olives, breadsticks, and spreads (see page 172 for more ideas). Make sure you keep all the food in one central location, ideally where everyone can have a seat. Throw a few floor cushions or large pillows around the table for an even cozier feel. It's the perfect recipe for everyone to get comfy and relax.

The Décor: Add pretty garnishes like sprigs of fresh herbs and jewel-toned fruits, and keep things visually interesting by layering the food on either a number of small coordinating plates and platters or on one large showstopper of a tray or board. Lower the lights, scatter some candles throughout the room, and play whatever music makes you feel like you're hanging out in your favorite cocktail lounge.

The Special Touch: No cocktail hour would be complete without drinks! A great way to get around having to fully stock your bar for a smaller gathering is to offer one signature cocktail. Round out the drink selection with red and white wine and your house beer of choice.

PICNIC IN THE PARK

MENU

Fried Chicken with Pickle & Potato Salad (page 81)

Sea Salt–Chocolate Chip Cookies (page 248)

Mango Sweet Tea (page 212)

I have such vivid memories of my mom breaking out the picnic blankets and vintage baskets, and packing up lunch or dinner for us to take to the park down the street. I can still see her in her huge round sunglasses—so '70s. We'd have so much fun running around, playing ball, and then coming back together to eat all the food she had made the night before. It was such precious family time, and I knew that when I had my own little family, we'd continue this tradition. Sure enough, packing up a meal for the park, beach, or lawn at Harper's school is one of our favorite ways to enjoy time together. A bunch of us gather, spread out our blankets, and lie around in the grass or sand munching on a potluck feast. Total Americana! I particularly love the idea of bringing something home-cooked, so I do this mom-style: prepped the night before so it's ready to go the next morning.

The Vibe: Nostalgic Summer Fun

The Food: My favorie menu is inspired by the classics. There's the don't-mess-with-the original fried chicken, plus potato salad updated with briny pickles and creamy eggs. For something sweet, pack up some Sea Salt–Chocolate Chip Cookies plus fresh fruit—like the biggest melon you can find so everyone can just dig in! No picnic is complete without a big pitcher of lemonade or iced tea, so I put my spin on an Arnold Palmer, but with mango juice instead of lemonade.

The Décor: This gathering is all about the atmosphere, so pick somewhere that's special to your family—the beach, a nearby park, a clearing near your favorite hiking trail, heck, even your backyard. Make sure to bring enough picnic blankets so there's enough room to set out the food and for everyone to sit. Flat bedsheets do great double-duty as blankets, especially if you're buying them just for this. Think mix-and-match but coordinating patterns in plaids, stripes, ginghams, and florals.

The Special Touch: Even though part of the fun of a picnic is keeping things super laid-back and casual, I like to add a few details that make it just the tiniest bit more polished. Napkin-lined baskets, glass jars for drinks, real plates and silverware (versus paper and plastic, if it's realistic!), plus platters and cutting boards will make it feel like you're bringing a little bit of your dining room outside.

NOW SHOWING...

THE PARENT TRAP

KIDS' MOVIE NIGHT

MENU

Salted Caramel Popcorn (page 188)

Maple Doughnut Holes (page 240)

Avocado Brownies (page 284)

Lucky Charms Bark (page 251)

Homemade Cherry Sodas (page 204)

Every once in a while, for an extra-special treat, we'll let Harper have a friend or two over to enjoy a super-decadent night where they can stay up late watching a movie and stuff themselves silly with yummy treats. Everyone dresses up in their favorite jammies, then we deck out the "viewing room" so it feels like their own special hideout—complete with lots of munchies and homemade sodas.

The Vibe: No Grown-Ups Allowed!

The Food: This spread takes the usual popcorn and candy up a notch.

The Décor: Transform your TV room into a special kids' hangout/home theater by decorating with things like string lights and lots of cozy throws and pillows for lounging (or for bouncing on and throwing—who are we kidding?!). Cover the windows with coordinating sheets, and if you're feeling super handy, create a canopy and temporary walls, too. Add a DIY movie marquee by using a chalkboard or felt boards, both of which you can easily find online, and for extra credit, add decorations that tie in the theme of the movie.

The Special Touch: To add to the indulgence of the night—as in, no bedtime and eating all the sugar you want!—I like to serve everyone their own homemade soda. It's incredibly simple to make and looks so sweet in old-fashioned glass bottles. Plus, it's just fruit, simple syrup, and seltzer, so you know you're not letting your kids load up on complete junk.

BACKYARD CAMP-OUT

MENU

Four-Bean Chili with Skillet Corn Bread & All the Fixins (page 93)

Campfire S'mores with Homemade Marshmallows (page 233)

Cabernet Sauvignon in a thermos

We can't get away for a proper camping trip every summer, so when we need a Great Outdoors fix, we throw a backyard camp-out with the kiddos.

The Vibe: State Park in Your Backyard

The Food: Rustic cookout classics like chili and s'mores are great for feeding a group—especially if you keep things DIY. Set out a big pot of the chili and bowls with all the fixins so people can make their own personalized bowl. The same goes for dessert: Arrange all the s'mores elements on a table and let guests help themselves. If you don't have a fire pit, bring things inside to use your fireplace, or use a handy-dandy kitchen torch. To add to the spirit of the evening, write on the invitation that it's "BYO thermos" and fill them up with everyone's beverage of choice. Have plenty of Cabernet or spiked hot cocoa for the grown-ups.

The Décor: I like to mix high and low for this party. Enamelware keeps things feeling casual and camp-y. Then add some finishing touches like tying utensil bundles with torn strands of flannel and, if it's windy, using rocks as napkin weights. Dot the tables with all-natural citronella candles to keep bugs away and also lend that signature smell of summer. Add pretty bunches of wildflowers to finish things off.

The Special Touch: Set up a tent for kids to play in, complete with flashlights or lanterns, and if it's in your budget, drape camping-style blankets over chairs so people can wrap themselves up if it gets chilly (you can usually find inexpensive options at discount stores). Then send your guests home with their own bag of homemade marshmallows.

ACKNOWLEDGMENTS

My Hubby: Brady, for always having an appetite, never saying no to doing the dishes, and loving me thru thick and thin.

My Kiddos: Harper & Holt, for being the loves of my life and creating memories alongside me in the kitchen.

My Family: Mom, Dad, Aunt, Uncle, and Tutu, for being such role models and teaching me the joy of cooking, gardening, entertaining, and art.

My Best Friend: Dean, for always being there and being my biggest cheerleader.

My Friends: for pulling up chairs at my table and being eager to feast on my food.

My Foodies: Jen, Ali, Santos, & Julie, for truly being my dream team and helping me create this book with love, beauty, and grace.

My Photographer: Rebecca, for always capturing special moments in my life so perfectly and with such beauty.

My Writer: Rachel, for your words of wisdom and guidance on this journey.

My Glam: Nicole, Michael, Junie, Rochelle, Candace, and Lucia, for truly making me feel beautiful inside and out and for making my family look so darn cute.

My Crew: Jai, Max, Ennis, Aron, Jonathan, Diandra, Nicole, Brandi, and Marc, for always having my back.

My Publisher: HMH, for making my dream of creating a cookbook into a reality.

My Inspiration: Maili, for being a dear friend and reminding me of my joy and love of food and cooking.

My Right Hand: Tory, for being so many roles in my life and doing them with such passion, grace, eagerness, joy, and love. I am so thankful for you coming into my life when you did.

Additional thanks to the many people who helped make this book happen: A.S.PaulJoy, All-Clad, American Heirloom Inc., Cardinal Food Service, Casa De Perrin, Cuisinart, Deborah Dupree, Facture Goods, Found Rentals, Jake Duke Rentals, Jono Pandolfi, KitchenAid, Le Creuset, Letterfolk, Messermeister, Nordic Ware, Orin Swift, Pottery Barn, Reese Supply Co., Robert Siegel Studio, Serax, The Petal Workshop, Tilt Aprons, Umami Mart, and Williams-Sonoma.

INDEX